Dissertation Solutions

A Concise Guide to Planning, Implementing, and Surviving the Dissertation Process

Bradley N. Axelrod and James Windell

ROWMAN & LITTLEFIELD EDUCATION
A division of
ROWMAN & LITTLEFIELD PUBLISHERS, INC.
Lanham • New York • Toronto • Plymouth, UK

Published by Rowman & Littlefield Education
A division of Rowman & Littlefield Publishers, Inc.
A wholly owned subsidary of The Rowman & Littlefield Publishing Group, Inc.
4501 Forbes Boulevard, Suite 200, Lanham, Maryland 20706
www.rowman.com

10 Thornbury Road, Plymouth PL6 7PP, United Kingdom

British Library Cataloguing in Publication Information Available

Library of Congress Cataloging-in-Publication Data

Axelrod, Bradley N., 1961-
Dissertation solutions : a concise guide to planning, implementing, and surviving the dissertation process / Bradley N. Axelrod and James Windell.
p. cm.
Includes bibliographical references.
ISBN 978-1-61048-867-9 (pbk. : alk. paper) -- ISBN 978-1-61048-868-6 (electronic)
1. Dissertations, Academic--Handbooks, manuals, etc. 2. Proposal writing in research--Handbooks, manuals, etc. 3. Academic writing--Handbooks, manuals, etc. I. Windell, James, 1940- II. Title.
LB2369.A94 2012
808.06'6378--dc23
2012028665

The paper used in this publication meets the minimum requirements of American National Standard for Information Sciences Permanence of Paper for Printed Library Materials, ANSI/NISO Z39.48-1992.

Printed in the United States of America

To Robin, my best friend and loving wife.
—B. N. A.

To Jane, my adorable wife.
—J. W.

Contents

Acknowledgments

This book would not be possible without the contributions of many people. In particular, we were fortunate to be able to draw on the experiences—both positive and negative—of many graduate students, interns, and former graduate students who have now attained their PhDs.

Although it is not possible to list every person who helped us in one way or another, we would be remiss to fail to acknowledge the help of the following people: Aaron D. Anderson; Douglas Campbell, PhD; Anne M. Conway; Julia Delektra, M.A.; Patricia B. Espe-Pfeifer; Jeffrey Evans, PhD; Melissa Grey, PhD; Joseph F. Kulas, PhD; Greg J. Lamberty, PhD; Scott W. Larson, PhD; Anthony Lequerica, PhD; Samuel Liebman, PhD; Mary Mahrou, PhD; Sylvia Malcore, PhD; Tamara McKay, PhD; Deborah Meizlish; Steve T. Michael, M.A.; Jenn Raiter, PhD; Lisa J. Rapport, PhD; Gregory Spence-Jones, PhD; David P. Sandrow; Nicole Tacoma, PhD; and Lily Trewhella, M.A. Each of these individuals shared their troubles and triumphs as graduate students on the way to completing their dissertations.

In addition, we want to thank Laurie Miller, M.A.; Elizabeth Hill, PhD; Pamela E. May, M.A.; and Joseph Ryan, PhD; all of whom were kind enough to read portions of the book, refer graduate students we could interview, or make valuable suggestions for revising chapters.

Finally, we thank our families (Robin, Robert, Ari; Jane) who support our professional work with the same vigor as they do our home lives.

Introduction

Oh boy! Now you have really done it! You decided to go ahead and get an advanced degree. You may have realized that you would need to do a dissertation and even a formal research project, but you were not aware of what that would entail. Sure, your professors, advisers, classmates, and friends have told you what they think you should do. However, that is a far cry from actually jumping in and understanding all the potential ins and outs of the dissertation process.

Thus far in your graduate education you have attended classes, completed assignments, and done what every instructor requested. You already know that your master's thesis or your doctoral dissertation will be unlike any other project you've ever taken on. And you certainly have an inkling that it will be more time-consuming than any of the projects you have completed so far. But, it is different in other ways as well. Our goal in this book is to make the whole process of planning, researching, and writing your dissertation a little more manageable.

Most important, if you are required to do a research project as part of your dissertation then it will be work that will be of your own choosing—or it will be work that is conducted with the assistance of your faculty adviser. You will, however, need approval for almost all aspects of your study.

Provided that your study is deemed acceptable, you will be doing the background reading, study design, data collection, statistical analyses, and formal write-up of an area that you have selected. In addition, you will be working on a schedule that is somewhat of your own making. That is, you will do the reading and writing, find the participants, create your database, and otherwise meet all of the needs of your study at your own rate. Many people at this point in their graduate education find this flexibility quite liberating.

But all is not a bed of roses. There are a number of obstacles that you will need to overcome to achieve the final goal of completing your research project, thesis, or dissertation. Just as in many video games, each step of the process has some hidden trap, and around every corner lurks some kind of obstacle. Although not mortally fatal, the threats that exist could certainly kill one's spirit and enthusiasm for completing the degree. Wouldn't it be wonderful if you could learn about the hazards in the complete dissertation process as easily as you can pick up the magazines written for video game solutions or Smartphone apps for game cheats?

Although we are not able to find you a quick "cheat" to give you the fast solution, our intent is to get you on the right track. We would like this book to be a manual and a guideline that will let you know about the roadblocks, traps, landmines, and hazards that could delay your ultimate goal of finishing a dissertation.

The purpose of this book is to give you some of the basic tools and tricks of the trade to get you through the process with minimal hassle. A golfer can't avoid landing in a sand trap or some other hazard. But, with the right knowledge, the golfer will avoid the hazard . . . or know how to get out of it quickly. Similarly, this text will not be able to prevent you from encountering the hazards that present themselves in the process of writing a proposal, finishing the dissertation, and getting it accepted as the final step in earning your PhD However, our goal is to pass along sufficient information so that you will be able to identify the traps ahead of time, avoid some of the hazards before they occur, and learn how to attack the most significant roadblocks directly and successfully.

In this book, we have selected a number of different topics that current and former graduate students presented to us. These areas are all sources of potential "derailment" in the dissertation process. The most heinous horror stories as well as the more mundane irritants are interspersed to serve as examples to learn from. You will find that the chapters are quite brief, as the goal was to present nuggets of relevant information. In most cases, the chapters can be read in any order as each one has information that is self-contained. If you have questions about forming a dissertation committee or dealing with your own procrastination, for instance, feel free to jump to that section and extract the needed information. The book is yours. How you use it is also up to you.

It may appear that many of the observations and suggestions that are contained in this book will seem quite logical and even obvious. Indeed, some things may be obvious to you because you are already familiar with those aspects of the process. In fact, you may already understand how to avoid or address one or more specific hassles within a graduate research or dissertation project. Of course, there could be several suggestions in this book that do not apply to you. If so, then gloss over them and focus instead on the chapters that offer you new information. Look to incorporate the information that applies to your current situation while spending less time focusing on chapters that seem simplistic for you.

There exist a number of excellent reference books that can provide detailed information about the preparation, execution, and writing of a dissertation project. This book does not intend to replicate those works, some of which we have listed as recommended readings. Rather than offering specific details for aspects of a dissertation project, we offer thoughts and suggestions about more global issues—and more practical issues—that hopefully will serve as a companion to more detailed books.

In addition to giving advice and ideas for getting started and completing your dissertation, this book we hope will inspire you with enthusiasm and the momentum required to begin the arduous task of your project.

Recently, we asked a current graduate student to review several chapters of our manuscript. Within hours, she returned the manuscript with a set of notes suggesting revisions. The next day, she was in her office in the hospital where she was doing an internship, typing furiously on her computer. She was asked what she was doing.

"Your book made me think about how I've been putting off even starting a proposal for my dissertation," She said. "I'm so inspired, that I'm determined now to get it done."

That is what we hope happens to you when you read our book. So let's get you in the mindset to begin focusing on your dissertation. Finding a topic, selecting a committee, designing a research study, analyzing the data, writing up the results, and offering a public presentation of your dissertation might seem like an awesome and daunting series of steps. But don't worry. We will take you through it step-by-step. We will motivate you to begin and then follow through with your project, and we will help you deal with the potential snags as they appear. You can do it.

Part I

Background

Chapter 1

It Isn't Simply Hazing

Academic research projects demonstrate mastery of a topic area and serve as a scientific contribution to the profession.

When you successfully complete your oral defense of a dissertation, committee members typically will say something like this to you: "Congratulations, Dr. Smith. Good work." What that means is this: "Congratulations, Dr. Smith. You have demonstrated that you are a critical thinker."

But, as you begin to address the mountain of work you have to face with your research project, it becomes quite easy to be cynical before accepting the accolade of being a great thinker. You might even become suspicious about the validity of this endeavor when you are having difficulty getting your proposal approved or coordinating a proposal date with your committee. We can imagine that you will be downright dubious about the utility of the whole thing when you begin to prepare your fifth "final revision" of your completed document.

Despite your protestations to the contrary, the purpose of an academic research project is not the implementation of educational sadism because your adviser had to suffer through the same experience.

Okay, so maybe you got saddled with the sadist. But we believe the great majority of faculty are fairly easy to work with, will be supportive, and will be dedicated to helping you complete your project and graduate. And the truth is, it is likely your research project will result in significant benefits both to the professional community and to you personally. You may be unaware of these benefits while you are in the throws of project revisions, data analyses, or conflicts with committee members. So, allow us to lay out the rewards to help extract some of the important positives this process will afford you.

The research process while in school allows you in vivo learning with the advantage of being in a somewhat protected setting. It is always better to be insulted by people who are your friends than by your enemies. While you are still in school, you are still with friends, believe it or not.

Your adviser and committee members serve as a symbolic cocoon for you before leaving the safety of the academic setting. Imagine if you did not have the presence of an advisory committee or academic colleagues. There is no doubt that some frustration experienced by students is related to irrational requests made by supervisors. You may not even believe that your adviser and committee members are guiding or protecting you in any way. However, by completion time, most graduates will agree that even the most seemingly unreasonable demands turned out to be for the better in the end.

Without the expertise of your adviser and committee members, your project might be disrupted at any step along the way. It is your committee members that help you find a topic area, direct you to appropriate reading, assist in formulating hypotheses to test, work to better define your study question, improve the methodology, decipher confusing data analyses, and edit your writing to improve its clarity and completeness.

One of the sayings from Confucius is, "I hear, I forget. I see, I understand. I do, I remember." In your research project leading to a thesis or dissertation, you will be experiencing trial by fire. Few ways of learning are better than trial by fire.

Jeffrey was jolted by his adviser when he was told—after waiting several weeks to hear back from his adviser about his research—that he needed to double the number of analyses that had been performed on the data. Recalling how difficult the analyses were the first time around, Jeffrey felt discouraged. However, following the advice of other students, he did what his adviser recommended.

To his complete surprise, Jeffrey ran all the analyses in one day, transferred the results to appropriate tables, and incorporated those tables into the results section. How was that possible, he was asked. "I think I learned a lot doing the analyses the first time," he said. "I surprised myself how quickly it all came back to me and how easy it was this time."

Regardless of the frustration experienced at the time, his prior experience with the analyses dramatically increased his understanding of conducting the computations the second time around. Certainly nobody wishes to tackle unreasonable requests. But, the good news is that the new information that you will be learning will become part of your knowledge base.

Completion of an academic research project demonstrates expertise in your knowledge of profession-related research. These skills are quite important even if you do not intend to pursue research as a significant aspect of your career. As a professional, you must be able to read published material in your field with a critical eye. This type of careful reading is different from the automatic acceptance of information that is presented in the written format most of us read as undergraduates. In fact, you likely have read all of the accepted existing literature published in texts over the course of your tenure. By the time you have reached the end of your educational experience, most materials will be in the form of articles and professional papers.

However, even published articles can be based on faulty assumptions or bad science. As an educated reader, you will need to evaluate manuscripts for such flaws rather than accepting the information at face value. Taking this type of analytic expertise one step further, you are now a member of the professional community. As a professional, you need to question as well as offer new ideas. Your knowledge will come into play in your professional life when you review research articles for journals, provide feedback on research proposals for colleagues, or merely engage in spirited professional reading for continuing education purposes.

But there are additional benefits afforded by doing your first major research project while still in school. You enjoy the camaraderie of others in the same situation, the professional support of individuals working on similar studies, the institutional backing needed in seeking funding, a place to do the research, and in some cases, even the equipment and supplies.

By doing this research project and writing your thesis or dissertation, you will become the expert. By the end of your project, you will be more familiar with your topic area than most other people. Whether your project requires data analysis or not, your final written product and oral defense will demonstrate your mastery of the specialty area you chose to study. Sure there might be a few people who have published extensively in the area, but you will be the resident authority on the topic.

As the maven, you will soon realize strengths and weaknesses of that area, as well as other studies that are conducted. You have made the climb from educated consumer to contributing scientific professional whom others might seek out for information. This change in professional identity will be made even clearer when you present your study at a professional meeting or other forum.

And now for the intangible benefits, the warm fuzzies that are otherwise difficult to operationally define. Before we talk about those, let us back up a bit.

A research study is the definitive learning experience. Prior to doing this type of work, academic studies likely have been regimented. Readings were assigned. Discussions were held. Lectures were attended. In terms of demonstrating your new-found knowledge, you took examinations, wrote papers, and presented information to others. Usually these tasks were all accomplished within a single semester. In addition, the material was learned and tested with others at that same time. Now it is time to do a research project. There are few timetables, little structure, few guidelines, and no group work.

Successful completion of the project requires a lot from you. In particular, you will certainly learn the practical aspects of evaluating an idea objectively.

In addition, by the time you have worked on the research project to its completion, you will have demonstrated other attributes. You will have shown motivation to begin such a multifaceted project and persistence in overcoming the ups and downs you are sure to have encountered. Your diligence will demonstrate your serious commitment to the field and to your studies. So by the completion of your research project, you will have both contributed to the professional world and learned to do so as a professional. By then, the words "Congratulations Dr. Smith. You are a critical thinker" will be well deserved.

Chapter 2

The Dissertation Process

The procedures from the inception of a project through its formal defense remain consistent across most academic institutions.

As a wide-eyed graduate student, you may only be vaguely aware of the process of a master's thesis or a doctoral dissertation. In spite of your general understanding that graduation requires completion of a thesis or dissertation, which might involve an independent research project, you may have been totally naïve as to the procedures involved.

Brad's first exposure to information he thought would improve his research knowledge was obtained in a research seminar, explicitly intended for first year graduate students. The information he and other graduate students attending the lecture were given was completely and utterly false. Of course he did not know that at the time. However, because the information that he was told was so vague, backward in logic, and full of assumed knowledge, the lecture only served to increase Brad's level of anxiety and confusion.

In brief, an associate professor, who soon thereafter was promoted to full professor, provided the following ridiculous information on how to write a research proposal:

> The first thing that you need to do is select a title. It should be long enough to explain the study while remaining short enough to keep the interest of the reader. You may use a colon in title if you wish, but try not to do so. You may also use a question mark, but again, this is frowned upon.
>
> The next area you will come to is the abstract. Here your responsibility is to summarize the work that you will do, the results you will obtain, and the meaning of those results as they relate to the background of your study. Avoid pointing out weaknesses of your study at this point. Most abstracts are short because they summarize all of the remaining information in the proposal that you have yet to write.

The introduction section, which is longer than the abstract, shows the reader that you understand the topic area and will be able to answer any questions about it. Make sure that you cite enough studies that explain what has been done without being over inclusive. On the other hand, do not have too few studies. That would only be seen as being incomplete. The articles you present in this section should be summarized completely without being plagiarized, and without being overly detailed or overly succinct.

And on it went. After 45 minutes of that kind of lecture, Brad was terrified. It was not until at least 18 months later that he realized how foolish this introductory lecture to research had been. Toward the end of Brad's second year as a graduate student, he finally had a supervisor who introduced him to a more practical approach to putting together a research proposal. Only then did it become clear that an abstract and title might be the *last* things that he would write in composing a research proposal rather than the *first* writing that he would do.

With the above story in mind, we would like to explain in reasonable terms the major steps required by most research projects. This information is most likely detailed by your graduate school or program in a formal, multipage document. Rather than preempt that document, we will provide the general structure. Your responsibility is to determine what alterations you will need to make because of specifications unique to your setting. In addition to your school's document that explicates the regulations of the proposal and the formal write-up requirements, current students are another excellent source of information.

So, to respond to your first anticipated question, the answer is "No, we don't know how many pages your thesis or dissertation has to be." And, "No, we don't know how long it will take you to get through your specific project." There is no better way to understand what is required by your specific school than by speaking with students who are a few years ahead of you in the program. In addition, use existing proposals or completed theses or dissertations from former students as guides. Typically, most schools keep copies of all theses and dissertations in the department as well as in the library.

Putting a research project together is a dynamic process and does not necessarily follow a specific order. As a result, the order in which you address each of the following tasks may change depending on your adviser or your school. All of these caveats aside, there is a common framework that is followed. Furthermore, some of the steps we give you in this chapter might actually be accomplished concurrently. Also, many of these steps are discussed in detail at other points in this book. So use this list as an opportunity to get an overview of what you are up against—and what you should expect with the dissertation process. Let's get to it.

1. Select a topic: There is no specific way to select a topic for your project. Various students decide on a topic in widely different ways. Sometimes they find an area of interest based on their reading of course materials, attending conferences, listening to current teachers, discussing research with colleagues, or learning with practicum advisers. Some have had personal experiences that have led them to become interested in a topic area. Others just stumble on an area that really fascinates them.

2. Select an adviser: This individual will be your most important information resource, guide, statistician, editor, and negotiator. Your adviser will help you generate an idea based on a topic area, or will offer you an opportunity to work within the research area of interest to them.

3. Formulate an idea: Generate and design a specific project with the assistance of your adviser.

4. Form a committee: With the assistance of your adviser and advice from other students, you will form a committee that will represent the department, the school, and the professional field.

5. Research the literature: You will see that the next step requires you to provide background information for your study. This stage necessitates bibliographic research time, searching, reading, summarizing, and understanding existing studies. This information will be the basis of your literature review in the proposal.

6. Write the proposal: This is your rationale and plan for your dissertation and your research project. Your job is to create a document that provides sufficient background and justification for the study, as well as outlining the way in which you will collect and analyze the information you are seeking to examine.

7. The written proposal is broken into a number of components. The *literature review* summarizes existing literature that is relevant for your topic area, concluding with works that set up the reader to be prepared for your study. At this point, you are outlining prior research, highlighting how those studies have advanced a particular area, and setting up the reader to understand where previous research has left off with other questions yet to be answered. The *statement of the problem* conceptualizes the material that seems to be lacking in the scientific literature. *Hypotheses* offer the specific questions that your study is trying to answer.

8. The *Method* section is typically broken down into subsections that describe the *participants* your study will use, the *instruments* to be applied, the *procedure* in which the participants will be subject to the instruments, and the *statistical analyses* you will perform on the resulting data.

9. Get approval from your adviser: It is your proposal that your adviser will ask you to write and rewrite, prior to getting your proposal approved, and all of this happens before you begin collecting any data for a research project. The revisions could focus on the background articles that you present

in the introduction or they may pertain to revising the design of the study. (It is around this time that a general concept or title for the study can be created, because the topic to be addressed will have been determined.)

10. Get approval from your committee: Once your proposal is written, it is time to hand it off to your committee members. Depending on your school, this may be done informally or it may require a formal proposal defense. This defense is an opportunity to publicly describe the background and design of the study. As with your committee chair, the members of the committee might request alterations in background information or in the design of the actual project.

11. Get approval from the Institutional Review Board (IRB): Whether it is the IRB for your school or for the facility where the participants are located, your project will undergo additional scrutiny. The purpose of this review is to ensure that your study is in compliance with the ethical and legal standards of the facility. Compliance pertains to how study participants will be treated as well as the broader question of how the data will be collected, stored, and retained following completion of the study.

12. Collect data: Whether your data collection is archival or with live participants, you should have already received written approval to use the information. That step is probably required by your committee or the IRB. After your project is approved by everyone who needs to approve it, it will be time to collect your data.

13. Score, code, enter, and analyze the data: These are the steps that will take the meat of your study from an individual's performance to an explanation of group data. The core hypotheses asked in your proposal are answered through these analyses. Often, your adviser will wish to be apprised of these results. Some advisers like to know your results by examining the printout of the analyses, while others do not want to look at the results until they are included in a draft of the results section for your final document.

14. More writing: After successful completion of data collection and analysis, there is nothing left to do but write your results and discussion sections. Often the results section will require the completion of tables in addition to the text.

15. More supervision: Your adviser and the committee will examine final drafts of your write-up. Your adviser will inform you as to when to schedule your defense, but your supervisor or adviser will play a large role throughout the process by discussing with you all—or nearly all—of these 17 steps.

16. Defense: Schedule your public defense with your committee, your department, and the school. Your actual public defense will vary across institutions. Regardless of where you are, you likely will be asked to present your study, highlighting its rationale, methods, and findings. After your presentation, the committee and others present will ask questions about aspects of your study and the findings.

17. Post-defense: In addition to basking in the afterglow of completing your project, you will be asked by your adviser and your committee to submit your project for presentation at a conference or for publication in a professional journal. The document, although already written, will need to be revised to conform to the requirements of the specific conference or journal.

These are the 17 basic steps necessary for you to complete. Make a checklist and start checking off the tasks as you complete them. Now that you've been provided with an overview of the whole process, put things in perspective. It's only 17 steps, and most of those are on the front end, before you begin collecting any data. You're going to get support and help not only from us in this book, but you're going to have the support and encouragement of your adviser, your committee, family, friends, and colleagues. With all this support and help, look at the project in a new way: This is something you *can* do.

Part II

Before, During, and After the Dissertation

Chapter 3

Don't Fear Starting

Begin your project RIGHT NOW! Do not wait for the perfect place, time, mood, idea, or written phrase as motivation.

In the book *Writing the Doctoral Dissertation: A Systematic Approach*, authors Davis and Parker provided research on the length of time most dissertations take from inception to completion. Their data found that most graduate student researchers take one to two years to complete their project. The median length of time is 15 months, with over 80 percent finishing by 18 months. We can almost hear the gasps and groans, with graduate students saying softly to themselves in disbelief, "One and one-half years?" With a comment like that, you will soon be overcome by the length of time required and the amount of commitment to the task needed.

Okay. So let's put it all out there. Davis and Parker also reported that by the time the dissertation is completed, the student will have taken four hours to generate each double-spaced page of text. So now you have two choices. Some students will bemoan the enormity of the project, instead electing to take a few more classes, another practicum, or taking on a teaching assistant position for an additional year. Others will place the quantity of work in perspective, accept this information as a guideline, and begin to make plans to tackle their dissertation sooner rather than later.

When thinking about the time commitment that you will make, it certainly becomes easy to be put off by this daunting task. Although it is quite obvious that any journey begins with a first step, it is interesting that when a "journey" becomes figurative rather than literal, the wisdom of this comment is lost. There exist a number of beginnings in getting a research project off the ground. These tasks include generating an idea, performing a literature review, summarizing the literature found, and so on. But none of these tasks will happen until you begin working.

Students and early researchers will create reasons for why they should not yet begin work on the project. Often arbitrary dates (e.g., "I'll wait until my birthday"), personally defined goals (e.g., after this semester), or perceived inadequacies in their abilities (e.g., "I'll wait until after I take my next statistics class") are used to delay the start of a project. In addition, most people are overwhelmed by a daunting task such as researching and writing a dissertation. When we get overwhelmed, we tend to shut down. So it is with many graduate students. As is the case with so many things, there never exists the best time or the right motivation to actually begin this awe-inspiring task.

The reality remains that the only good time to begin your work is right now. Delaying for any of the reasons stated above simply means that you are procrastinating. When it comes to writing projects many people, students included, think about large blocks of time they will need to get started. However, no matter the reason for your procrastination, the size of the project doesn't become smaller or easier. Since the project remains the same, only the time you begin it will change. Once you begin working on your project, you will notice that you have overcome one of your biggest obstacles.

As you sit down to begin your first writing, it is easy to be intimidated by a stack of blank paper or an empty computer screen with a flashing cursor. Graduate students will complain after hours of staring at emptiness, "I don't know how to start." It is at times like these, when experiencing a writer's block, that the wisdom of "writing anything" comes into play. The benefit of writing your own document is that you do not need to start at the beginning. You do not need to generate a pristine document the first time through. So if you do not know how to write the first sentence, skip it for now. Move onto the second sentence, another paragraph, or a different section. If it's easier to begin by writing a reference list, then do so. Because once you have written something, it becomes much easier to write something else.

Alternatively, you can attempt to begin writing at the beginning of what will be your final document, rather than simply the sections that might come more easily. But do so with the idea that you might not even use any of the first few pages written. The purpose at this point is to get the ideas out on paper, even if they are not yet well conceived. It is always easier to revise text than it is to generate text. Be that as it may, the ever-presence of word processing has spoiled us into thinking that when a document is printed or saved, it is in close to final form.

Back in the olden days of typewriters, pen, and paper, notes in the margins, lines scribbled out, lines with x's marked through them, as well as other notations clearly demonstrated that a work was a draft. Word processing has certainly improved the visual clarity of our drafts. But the clarity has come with the price of assuming that if a document is pristine, then it should be close to final form.

It may seem relatively easy to sit in front of the same paragraph and rewrite it for an afternoon. But by doing so, you will have spent your time *editing* and not *writing*. In order to get started, the novice writer should make a serious attempt at writing that is more along the lines of stream of consciousness than it is professional writing.

The goal at the beginning stages is to demonstrate to yourself that it is possible to get started. Moreover, even written material that you will not use in your final product allows you to better conceptualize the material that you have already pulled together. You will soon notice that you are interested in getting to the next stage, and the memory of having difficulty beginning will be distant.

Chapter 4

Get It Out of the Box—
Work on It Early and Often

Working regularly for short times leads to increased project familiarity and diminished dissertation-related guilt.

During the 1960 presidential election, Chicago's Mayor Richard J. Daley was a strong supporter of John F. Kennedy. As the story goes, his suggestion to the people of Chicago was "vote early and often." Mayor Daley was criticized for his remark because of the implication of corruption—primarily because of the "often" comment as opposed to the "early." Nonetheless, his comment certainly applies to working on any long-term project. As we have said once before in this book, you should begin working on your project sooner rather than later. More important, keep your ideas fresh by working on your study as regularly as possible.

THINKING THAT LEADS TO PROCRASTINATION

Some people are deluded into thinking that if they are working on a large project then large portions of time need to be set aside to make significant headway. It certainly seems that setting aside a chunk of time might bode well for getting much accomplished on a project. However, when you think that way, it becomes very easy to leave the work for the next day, or for the weekend, or for winter break. But, the reality remains that the longer you distance yourself from your work, the more difficult it becomes to get back into the rhythm of the work.

Many graduate students doing a research project deceive themselves into thinking that they will analyze their data and write their dissertation while on a one-year clinical internship or during winter break. This is the way some students think: "My data are already collected. I'll very easily be able to analyze the data and get the writing knocked out in a matter of months. In fact, I have a whole year to work on it. So, if it takes more that a few months, that won't be a problem either."

But what happens? They begin working full-time at their internship, sometimes even staying longer. Or they get involved in their current classes. Or they take on a part-time job. After a long day of work or classes, no one is all that interested in cracking open the taped box of articles or the file that contains the data. Add the additional stressors individuals experience if they have relocated to a new area and are trying to get used to a new environment.

After one or two months, it becomes increasingly easier to think of reasons as to why one shouldn't work on the project rather than pushing up one's sleeves and merely beginning. By this time, beginning has become the greatest challenge one needs to surmount.

It is interesting how many individuals share the same sentiment about their inability to get their project started. A number of excuses are initially presented. However, the end result is always the same. It becomes too difficult to begin working on a project that has remained untouched. Consequently, the pile of articles becomes a stagnant stack of papers that begins to feel like an immovable unitary entity. The more time that passes, the more your work will feel like an albatross. So, you need to make your project less stagnant and less "dead." In this case, absence does *not* make the heart grow fonder.

TAKE THE FIRST STEP

The first step to making your project a living project is to take the materials out of the box. That box may be in the closet or under other boxes. Or it might be out in the open taunting you to get started. If you are not using paper, then get those pdfs of your research articles into a subdirectory that you will actually open. Better yet, save them to your desktop as a constant reminder of what you are working on.

It may sound foolish, but unless you use your materials on a regular basis, you will only see them as a singular object or a project that needs to be completed. However, a project is made up of small parts—individual research articles to be read, data to be coordinated and analyzed, an outline to be filled with narrative. By breaking down the large project into its components, the required tasks begin to take on a more manageable quality.

BIG BLOCKS OF TIME ARE NOT NECESSARY IN ORDER TO MAKE SIGNIFICANT PROGRESS

"I can't get started unless I have several hours to devote to this. As soon as I have three or four hours one day to work on this, I'll get started." That's one of the things that your brain tells you when you are avoiding work on your project.

You know about cognitive distortions, right? Well, this is one of them. The truth is that you need to work on your study regularly and not only when large periods of time are available. In fact, given the lifestyle and time commitments of most graduate students, there will rarely be those days when you have several hours to commit to your project. Working a little at a time leads to sustained familiarity with your project and also reduces self-induced dissertation-related guilt.

There is a parable that might be helpful in its application to this concept. The story is of a bewitched troll who is housed in a castle on a mountain that can only be accessed by ascending hundreds of stairs that are set into the mountain. The troll challenges the kingdom that he will turn the throne over to whoever can jump to the castle at the top of the mountain. Of course, the unwise adults attempt to make the grand jump to the top of the mountain. Time and again they fail, ending up injured or in brambles that are planted on the mountain.

Then, a young boy approaches the mountain. He jumps from the ground to the first step. Then, he jumps from the first step to the next step. He continues in this manner, jumping one step at a time until he reaches the summit of the mountain and confronts the troll. The troll smiles knowingly. "You are correct," the troll says to the young boy. "I never stated that you had to make it to the top of the mountain in a *single* jump."

The moral, which may seem obvious, is that there is no requirement that your *entire* project be completed at one time. Take the advice from the wise child in the story, and work on it a little at a time.

WORK AT IT IN LITTLE CHUNKS

Got dissertation block? Thesis fear? Project avoidance? Our advice is to chunk it. Work in small chunks of time.

If you have 30 minutes available, open the box and make small stacks of what you need to do. Going to the doctor's office for an appointment? You know you'll be sitting in the waiting room for at least 20 minutes, maybe longer. Take one or two research articles and a highlighter. Read those articles instead of a year-old issue of *Time* magazine or the latest goings on with

your social network friends. Going to heat up a frozen meal in the micro-
wave? That sounds like you could have up to 15 minutes of time. Use that
chunk of time to outline or jot down what you're going to do in the next week
in your chunks of time.

MAKE YOUR GOALS ACHIEVABLE

Your goals need to be achievable. It is well and good that individuals might
have a goal to complete the project before graduation or by a particular time
of year. However, the reality remains that there are too many unknown
challenges that you might confront to know whether such a goal is attainable.
Less lofty goals that are more specific are more attainable. And although the
ultimate target remains the same—jumping to the top of the castle—the
manner in which you get there should be significantly more reasonable.

When planning her dissertation work, Karina set what she thought was a
reasonable goal: "Complete the literature review in two months." Although
this goal is better than her initial goal to "Complete the dissertation in 14
months," it still lacked the specificity that we believe will be easier for you to
gauge your progress. At the recommendation of some of her classmates,
smaller objective steps were proposed to Karina in hopes that it would be
more motivating. She was told to "read two articles per week for the literature review."

That kind of goal was certainly less lofty. And yet, Karina recognized that
she would be more likely to find time every week to read at least two articles
than she would have been able to regularly schedule time to perform the
more obtuse "complete the literature review."

YOU CAN WORK BACKWARD FROM YOUR ULTIMATE GOAL

There are some individuals who will begin mapping out their project by
looking at the long-term goal, and then working backward to determine how
they will achieve that goal based on weekly goals and steps. If, for instance,
you know that you need to complete your literature review in 10 weeks, then
the amount of time set aside for research, reading, and writing can be more
easily defined. You can set minigoals for each week during this 10-week
time frame.

YOUR PROJECT IS AN ONGOING PROCESS

The goals that you set will certainly need to be refined and delineated on an ongoing basis. But, that is the key. *Ongoing* is the watch word. Take the lead from the tortoise in Aesop's tale: Slow and steady wins the race.

Chapter 5

Work Ahead

Extra time is better spent beginning the next stage in your dissertation than it is
scheduling relaxation and entertainment.

When requesting advice and suggestions from neophyte researchers, we were
struck by a recurring recommendation by these recent graduates emphatically
stating the need for regularly scheduled entertainment. Clearly stated, these
souls believe that nonstop work on a dissertation requires planned breaks to
maintain one's sanity during the dissertation process. Let's be clear at the
outset; we do not agree with this position as we believe that continued chipping away at your project will be the most effective way in getting the project
completed.

A VACATION FROM YOUR PROJECT IS COUNTERPRODUCTIVE

We do not propose that you work 16 hours per day on your dissertation.
Instead, we are raising the point that you should not take a *hiatus* from your
work. Most important, it is exceedingly rare that a graduate student has so
many activities scheduled for the dissertation that they are otherwise unable
to have any free time. We might tip our hand and say, "Okay, go ahead and
schedule recreation, but only after you have first scheduled all of the time
devoted to the research project." In other words, you can take a yoga class
regularly for health and relaxation, but not to avoid working on your dissertation.

There is, they may point out, the old proverb that says that "All work and
no play makes Jack a dull boy." Since that first was written in the 17th
century, apparently a great many people have found wisdom in this saying. It

might be conceded that the research product and the quality of life will become stale if students spend all of their waking hours working on their dissertation. In addition, there is the notion that down time is required to regroup cognitively before you attack your work the following day.

A number of recent students stated that their salvation in working on their dissertation was scheduled time to participate in recreational activities. "Yoga!" shouted one student. "To the mall!" cried another. Regardless of the destination, most of these graduates claimed that students need to regularly plan opportunities for exercise, movie rentals, movie theaters, restaurants, walks in the park, or dinner parties. Not only did former graduate students support this notion, but so do authors of other books on dissertation writing. As with the students, authors of those other books opine that students need to make time for relaxation and not spend all of their time working on their research.

Do not be mistaken, there is indeed something comforting in reading a book that is giving you permission to take time off. You might even experience a sense of relief when explicitly sanctioned to take a break when you are working on your dissertation. What could be better than a mandate to go to a movie, exercise, eat out for dinner, or otherwise *not* work on your dissertation?

But let's face facts. It may well be that individuals who need to be told they ought to schedule "Rest and Relaxation" are probably not reading this book. Those individuals are dutifully reading, writing, analyzing, and performing other activities that are bringing them closer to completion of the project.

RELAXATION AND REST ARE GOOD, BUT . . .

We admit relaxation and rest are good. However, the need to schedule forced relaxation does not have a genuine ring to it. Most individuals working on their dissertation do not participate in "excessive work." In fact, the contrary typically occurs in which weeks will go by and the project remains untouched. Certainly there are times when the work can be more intensive. For example, when reading numerous articles, writing the literature review, or analyzing data one could easily find enough to do that would keep you busy around the clock. More often, you will experience long delays between stages of your research. Here are examples of just a handful of delays that you might experience:

• Waiting for feedback from your adviser regarding preliminary analyses

- Awaiting your adviser's or committee's review at any number of stages of writing
- Waiting for the schedule for the Institutional Review Board (IRB) to review your proposal. Some IRBs only meet quarterly during the year.
- Awaiting the arrival of any test materials or equipment
- Planning, coordinating, and scheduling of participants or data collection sites
- Downtime when scheduled participants do not show up
- Delays between the time a meeting is scheduled and the actual date

It is these natural breaks in the action that will provide you with time to perform fewer activities relating to your dissertation. It is also during these times that you can reward yourself with some type of treat that you had not previously been able to do because you have been busily working on your project. Students will use the achievement of a specific goal (e.g., completing the literature review, defending the proposal) as a reason to take a break from working on the project.

BREAKS SHOULD BE LIMITED

The practice of giving yourself a hiatus from work as a reward can become counterproductive to progress unless you can set specific limits on the length of the break. Graduate students sometimes see these natural breaks as chances to give themselves a rest. The conflict arises when these breaks last more than a few days. Then, the procrastination discussed in Chapter 4 comes into play.

Use gaps in work activity to energize you for the next stage. Rather than seeking out opportunities to avoid working on your dissertation, you should seek out occasions to begin the next stage in your dissertation. There is always some next step that can be accomplished. For example, if you are waiting to hear back from a potential data collection site, use the time to consider a backup plan if you are denied. On the other hand, if you are only waiting for formal approval, then use the time to prepare for data collection. If you have already begun data collection, then use your R&R time to score, code, or enter your data into the appropriate database. If a draft of your literature review section is sitting with your adviser, then attack the method section. Even if there are revisions that will be made by your adviser, those revisions will still need to be made if you waited the few weeks until you heard "yea" or "nay" about the literature review.

In summary, rather than finding excuses to shop or grab a beer with friends (because there will *always* be time to do those things without putting them on a rigid schedule), keep working on what is in front of you—and also keep working on whatever the next step is for your study.

Chapter 6

Back It Up

Retain multiple backups of your documents in multiple physical and electronic locations.

Why is common sense so uncommon—at least in some areas of our personal lives? It is just common sense that we should eat or drink in moderation. That we should eat several fruits and vegetables every day. That we should not smoke. That we should save 10 percent of our income. That we should not text or talk on our cell phones while driving. That we should change the batteries in our smoke detectors twice annually.

And yet how many of us follow these commonsense dictums? For example, at a majority of fatal fires there are working smoke detectors at the scene that have either old batteries or have had the batteries removed. Logical, commonsense advice always applies in theory—but it is so easy to neglect applying it in our daily life.

With that premise in mind, everyone would agree that it makes practical sense to make copies of any work product that is as important as a dissertation. Wonderfully horrific stories exist about house fires and other disasters that destroyed all written material associated with a particular study. For instance, Ronald, a graduate student working on his PhD in biology, had his car stolen. Unfortunately, Ronald had the final draft of his dissertation in the trunk of the car. He didn't care if he ever saw the car again, but the draft of his dissertation was the only copy he had.

Pamela, another graduate student, had all of her research data on her laptop computer. While traveling, she left it in a taxicab—and never saw her laptop—or her valuable data again. Travis was carrying his data, including the original test results of several hundred subjects, in a box in the trunk of his car. He had not yet transferred the data to a computer. When he was broadsided at an intersection, his trunk sprang open, and the contents of his trunk went flying in every direction. Travis was injured and had to be transported by ambulance to the hospital, but all the ER physician heard about was the pain of losing his research.

Graduate students fearing the worst possible scenario have perfected ways of protecting their work. In the pre-computer "olden days" dissertation drafts were duplicated in the writing stages through the use of carbon paper. Alternatively, with the writing and rewriting of drafts, previous versions were retained in a separate location, just in case the more recent version got destroyed. Some pre-computer advisers recommended storing drafts of one's dissertation in the freezer compartment of the refrigerator. The thinking was that even if your apartment burned to the ground, you would be able to find a pristine copy of your dissertation within the sealed and melted blob of what used to be the refrigerator.

COMPUTERS MAKE STORAGE EASIER

Computers can certainly make copying and backing up information easier. But you cannot rely on the magic of technology to do its work without getting directly involved in the process. The advent of the home computer has not eliminated the need to carefully consider how you will personally back up your research information.

START WITH THE BASICS OF BACKUP

Let's start out in a simple way as we progress to maximizing resources in storing your information to minimize the impact of the feared doom and disaster of a lost file. First, most word processing programs allow for an automatic electronic backup, as well as a save command, both considered default programs. However, before disaster strikes it would be useful to see if you can actually retrieve the automatic backups. Have you ever tried to find the automatic backup files? They are often saved with indecipherable codes unless otherwise defined by the user. In addition, one can easily use the "save as" command to create a complete copy of the current file on the computer.

Okay, so now you have some type of backup on the computer hard drive. Consequently, if one section of the drive is corrupted or if the file is accidentally deleted, you still have access to the backup. However, does it really make sense to have multiple copies of a document on a single computer hard drive? Of course not, you say. Anyone with a glimmer of computer knowledge will recognize the foolishness of having the only copies, even if there are multiple copies, of a document on a single computer.

An electrical storm, a power surge, a stray cup of coffee, or any of a multitude of other potential disasters could knock out an entire computer without leaving hope for recovery of your document. So that means making backups of your information in multiple locations, such as on a couple of backup diskettes or flash drives after each session.

Bridgette, a third-year graduate student, was aware of the need to back up her information. She made it a point to back up her documents at home on a disk, and then on her computer at the office where she was working. Imagine her surprise when one day she found that the work computer had a virus that had attached itself to her document. Fortunately, she thought her personal computer at home still had a safe document. However, by shuttling her document back and forth, the virus was not only at work, but also on the disk and on her home computer. The only way she could save her document was to retype the entire dissertation proposal. Another unsuspecting graduate student was equally terrified of losing his information that had been stored electronically. Brian recognized the importance of backing up his data in multiple physical places. Consequently, whenever he worked on his dissertation, he concluded the session by compulsively copying his newest draft onto no less than six separate disks and flashdrives. Brian's bubble was burst when he was halfway through his backup process one day, and discovered that the original file had been corrupted with a virus. Not only had the original file been tainted by the virus, but all of the disks and flashdrives he had backed up his document on had also been infected. Fortunately for Brian, he had not completed his backup procedures, saving the last few disks from destruction.

These incidents should not dissuade you from using computers. However, they should put you on notice to carefully consider all options regardless of what backup system you adopt.

It is strongly recommended that you prepare for any possible electronic, natural, or man-made disaster. Consequently, it is recommend that all drafts are printed, so a hard copy of the most recent version is always available. Next, back up into two locations on the same computer hard drive, as well as onto another disk or flash drive. Other potential disks include floppy disks, zip disks, a burned CD, a network drive, or electronic storage with an Internet provider's storage space.

The final compulsive act, for use when you have completed a solid draft of a chapter or some other significant accomplishment, is to e-mail the document to yourself as an attachment. Don't open the file. Keep it in cyberspace. You will then be able to access it in the unlikely event that all other drafts get corrupted, deleted, or eaten by your dog.

Part III

Selecting Your Topic or Research Study

Chapter 7

Use Coursework Strategically

> Required coursework assignment projects can assist in formulating ideas, re-
> viewing literature, designing studies, and writing a proposal while imposing
> required deadlines on your production.

Many advanced graduate students and recent graduates have some sound
advice for graduate students about to embark on a dissertation. Their advice?
They recommend seeking out research projects that are of topical interest to
students. Their reasoning is as sound as their advice: if you like what you are
working on, then you will be more likely to remain active and involved in the
study.

Even if selecting a topic of interest does not result in a speedier completion of the study, you will be more likely to enjoy the time that you do spend
working on it. Think of your dissertation as you might a long cross-country
driving trip. Traveling with someone you enjoy spending time with may not
take less time on the clock to reach your goal. However, the trip will be more
enjoyable.

Academic courses provide an excellent source for generating ideas of
interest for a dissertation project. The more you study and learn related to the
field that interests you the most, the greater the chance that you are going to
learn things that will enhance your work on your dissertation project. There
is also a greater chance that you are going to generate new ideas, discover
that you can bring together two or more concepts in new or different ways, or
come up with a unique approach to your research or your writing.

There is an additional benefit of taking a number of classes before generating a specific study. Your classes expose you to a myriad of studies over a
number of courses in different topic areas of study. There are certainly academic subjects and clinical areas of interest that overlap. Much of the information presented in your coursework summarizes existing literature in a

particular topic area. In most cases, material presented by faculty is quite current, and readings are more often in the form of articles than they are in texts.

As you read these articles, pay attention to studies that are of interest to you or are projects that might be improved on. A research field may be interesting because of the topic of the study, sample studied, variables included, study design, or proposed areas of future research. With an eye on potential prospects for research, you will be able to evaluate possible opportunities for contribution while completing an assignment that is already required.

Specific homework that is assigned can offer the potential for serving two purposes. The first purpose would be to fulfill whatever course requirement the professor has. In addition, though, a literature review or a critique of a published study may provide a launching point for your dissertation. For example, if you are asked to address any topic area and provide a summary of existing research, that paper should be approached as if you are writing your dissertation literature review. In thinking this way, you will give yourself a jump-start on your actual research study's literature review.

Adam was interested in comparing different treatment methods in helping people stop smoking. He was considering that this could be a reasonable study that he might move forward into a dissertation. Rather than reading articles for the sole purpose of his dissertation, he decided to use a class assignment as the excuse of learning more. In his therapy class, the instructor wished students to summarize a therapy area. Adam used that opportunity to evaluate existing literature on smoking cessation, successfully completing his assignment while also learning about the field.

Similarly, research design classes sometimes request that you demonstrate your expertise by designing a study and setting forth proposed statistical analyses. Do not select a homework project based on a whim or because it will be easy to do. Instead, use the class as an opportunity to design an actual study based on what you believe your formal research project will actually be. Your preliminary write-up is a homework assignment. Your project will therefore be critiqued by the professor—and perhaps by other students. There is be no better time to get feedback from a project than at the very beginning. The grade you receive will be relatively minor in comparison to the support, alterations, weaknesses, and strengths noted by the teacher of that class.

Of course, you must be aware that your professor, your fellow students, or your adviser might not approve the ideas, literature review, or design of your studies. But, that's the benefit of early feedback. Other people may be in a much better position than you to see the flaws in your project. Others may be able to suggest a better study design or point out an important piece of literature that was previously omitted that should be included in the literature review.

Regardless of your adviser's concern, approaching your course assignments as potential elements of your formal research project will get you to the goal more quickly. Compare this approach to students who take classes and complete the required assignments without thinking about their research project or dissertation. They will begin their research study from scratch after all of the required courses are completed.

There is an additional benefit to working on a larger research study when taking your classes. Unlike a dissertation or thesis, a graduate course has specific timelines when materials need to be completed. Most of your dissertation work will be accomplished on your own time and without deadlines, except those that you apply arbitrarily. In contrast, professors dole out homework and usually assign a due date at the same time. These concrete deadlines are externally mandated, thereby forcing you to complete whatever aspect of the planning you are required to do in a timely manner. You can use such deadlines as an advantage to achieve whatever work you wish to accomplish toward your project. You will be living with self-imposed deadlines throughout your dissertation project. Getting used to meeting these deadlines will serve you well as you plan your project.

Chapter 8

Read Journals and Attend Conferences Aggressively

Use exposure to existing literature as an opportunity to generate research ideas.

Seeking out a study that will interest you usually serves as a good motivating factor. If you tend to be better motivated on tasks that interest you (which is probably true for most of us), then that fact should influence the types of projects you will seek out. Ideas can easily be generated by examining the limitations of published studies and improving on them. Research that expands or clarifies an existing theme has the benefit of beginning with a circumscribed topic area. In addition, its existing presentation speaks to the positive response that the field has to such a topic.

READ JOURNALS IN YOUR FIELD

From a practical perspective, check out the journals that tend to publish research that interests you (or your adviser). Create a relationship with those journals. Read regularly the tables of contents and corresponding articles that fall within your topic area. Once you have familiarized yourself with the topics, you will begin to take a more critical read through the articles. You should be reading for both the strengths and weaknesses in published studies, as well as thinking of new studies that might better test a particular hypothesis. This approach to the literature calls for you to look at studies as part of an integrated research program, not as unitary entities.

ATTEND LECTURES

We hope you love attending conferences. We do. And we love attending conferences because there is an exhilaration in the air when you are together with other individuals who have professional interests that are similar to your own. These individuals can be well-known researchers, less-known contributors who may be early in their career, or other students. No matter what reason you attend conferences, symposia, or workshops, and no matter what your specific interests, you should attend with one thought in mind: I'm going to come away from this conference with at least one new idea or exciting brainstorm that I am going to use.

For most of us, when we were younger and starting out our careers, attending that first professional meeting was exciting and overwhelming. There was a sense of exhilaration at being in the same room listening to a speech or presentation by someone you knew through the literature in your field. It is impressive—even for veterans in a field—to hear a well-known innovator of great theories or seminal research actually presenting their work in front of you. The excitement of these brushes with greatness soon can be replaced by an honest interest in the content of the material presented.

Getting beyond the excitement of listening to a live presentation by someone you have studied can allow you to generate your own ideas and thoughts about their work. In addition to presenting existing material, senior researchers will also present upcoming work. This previewing of material is possible because published material often takes two years from the time it is submitted until an article is printed in a journal. Consequently, conferences provide scholars the occasion to present recent theoretical shifts, new research, or novel hypotheses far in advance of their being published.

Experts in a particular field will present information altering their own published theories or introducing new ways to examine existing theories. This forum provides an excellent chance to observe opinion leaders questioning their own theories and methods for testing those theories. This is a wonderful opportunity for you and your own future research. Attending these sessions offers you a chance to come up with your own theories or research studies by listening to authoritative figures in the field. You really can experience this exhilaration by listening to the musings of a proven expert—especially when potential future research directions are offered.

Many of the presentations that make significant impact are first presented in conferences or workshop sessions in which the contributor presents his material in a speech with a slide show. Aside from those presentations, conferences also offer a forum to talk to researchers in a less formal setting.

In poster sessions, presenters summarize the findings of a particular study in a written format that is tacked onto a bulletin board for a period of time. Usually, there are dozens of other posters presented in the same session.

POSTER SESSIONS

During a poster session, conference attendees will stroll past the rows of bulletin boards, reading the research summaries that are of particular interest to them. This arrangement allows for many studies to be presented simultaneously. More importantly, though, researchers have the opportunity to respond to individual questions and speak with colleagues in a setting that is much less formal than a slide show presentation. This gives you a great opportunity to interact with professionals and it is more likely you will be able to speak one-on-one with an expert than if you are part of an audience when they are presenting their research in a formal setting.

Truth be told (and we know this from experience), it can be rather boring to stand in front of a bulletin board for two hours. That also means poster presenters are very eager to talk to anyone who has questions or comments about their poster. However, when you are the person asking questions, it is a chance to learn about their research and to talk privately—or almost privately—with someone who has done research in a field that may be of interest to you.

As a graduate student, you can use poster sessions to find particular studies that are of interest. If after reading the study your interest remains strong, use your time to speak with the author. Talk about strengths of the studies. Discuss challenges that alterations in a future study could avoid. Assess the possibility of expanding or enhancing the work. Ask about additional or companion research conducted by the author. In short, use these sessions to have informal conversations about specific professional areas that interest you.

The final major benefit of a conference, as far as dissertation research goes, is that you will meet other students and colleagues. What students lack in experience relative to established professionals is often entirely offset by a strong breadth of interests. It is through collegial relationships established with other students and junior colleagues that most ideas can be generated and modified. Conferences give you a forum to find out who else is interested in the type of work that interests you. It is quite common to feel more comfortable brainstorming ideas with fellow students than with established researchers. So, meet like-minded researchers and explore ways in which you can work together or at least support each other's work. Remember, in a few short years, these individuals will be your colleagues.

Chapter 9

Investigating Faculty Members' Research

Learn about a faculty member's research by reading prior studies and speaking with students who have worked with that individual.

A topic area for your dissertation can come from within your school or, in some cases, from another professional in the field who is affiliated with your school. Whether you consider the work or subject area of a current faculty member or an affiliated professional, your decision will need to be made after some effort on your part. In addition to learning about the type of research performed by faculty members, you will also evaluate the quality of their work, their ability to work with other students, and their interest in working with you. This is important in finding an adviser for your dissertation or when thinking about people you would like to have on your dissertation committee.

RESEARCH BY FACULTY

Let us first examine how to learn about the research conducted by faculty. Many schools offer seminars to graduate students where current faculty and affiliated professionals informally present their research. These sessions offer a great opportunity to hear these individuals speak, grasp the type of work they typically perform, ask questions, and see how they respond to queries about their work. Unfortunately, these seminars usually occur early in most graduate programs, when the students have not yet begun thinking about a research project. If this was the case with you, then I would speculate that you and your classmates sat through those sessions thinking about the course work that you would have preferred to be working on or the other nonacademic activities you would rather be doing.

Actually, that was probably reasonable at that time. However, now that you are ready to learn about what opportunities might exist, the lectures are being given to fellow students who are much more junior than you arc. So although you may even have a good sense of the research of a particular professional, it is time to attempt to reconnect, and gain a better and more current perspective from that person.

The best approach to this step is to ask the faculty member for a few reprints of articles that summarize some of their recent studies. This is a much better tactic then asking, "What is your research about?" By reviewing reprints, you will get a good look at the types of projects completed and the subject matter that is of particular interest for this faculty member. Although it may seem self-evident, the studies that are of greatest interest to the potential adviser are going to be the ones that are forwarded to you in the form of a past publication.

Many researchers have a variety of interests. Getting involved with topics that have a good track record with a researcher will likely be a better bet than pursuing areas that are of ancillary interest to the potential adviser.

A scenario that proves to be less promising is to try to find a faculty member who will chair an idea that you generated on your own. Regardless of the originality or quality of your study, you will place yourself in the complex position of trying to either teach a faculty member or generate enthusiasm in a research area that heretofore had not been of interest to that faculty member.

By reviewing prior publications in a faculty member's topic area, you will also begin to assess the do-ability of a study. In particular, you will wish to pay attention to the participants that are usually included in the studies, the types of measures used, the complexity of the study designs, and the quality of the statistical analyses employed.

Research that consistently employs atypical or difficult-to-find participants will raise a very appropriate concern—that your project might take longer to complete than other studies with which they could be involved. Similarly, if you believe that the study designs or data analyses normally used by the research team seem too cumbersome for you, it is better to evaluate that now rather than after you have created a literature review and written a proposal.

Some faculty members create a research team composed of graduate students who are all working on projects with that individual. Research team meetings then allow for all of the graduate students to summarize their accomplishments, practice their research defense presentations, and otherwise interact with graduate students with the same general interests.

EVALUATING FACULTY AS POTENTIAL CANDIDATES FOR YOUR DISSERTATION ADVISER

When evaluating potential advisers, request that you be allowed to attend any research team meetings that might take place. The potential of becoming active in an existing research program has the benefit of allowing you to work with fellow students on established projects within a circumscribed body of research. In addition, you will get the inside story with regard to the adviser and potential committee members. The support from fellow students is also realized by attending each other's proposal and defense meetings.

An additional benefit of reviewing papers that a faculty member has published or presented at professional conferences is the collaborative nature of the instructor's relationship with the students. Does the adviser include graduate students as coauthors on professional papers and publications? When members of the research team appear as coauthors on more than one article, the greater the likelihood that the research process is collaborative. Furthermore, it demonstrates that the faculty member truly views the graduate students as part of a team in which publications are products of the entire team and not of an individual.

This is not to say that the only potential working relationship is within a team framework. Rather, if you are one who would prefer that type of research environment, then this aspect in reviewing publications is of relevance.

WOULD THIS FACULTY MEMBER BE WILLING TO WORK WITH YOU?

Finally, is the faculty member interested in working with you? Of course, the true test will be when the discussions about working on specific projects become serious. In the meantime, their interest in working with you might be gleaned by how responsive they are to your requests for reprints, observation at a research team meeting, and availability to discuss past research (and future possibilities) with you. In essence, it is suggested that you approach a potential adviser as you might an employer. Evaluate the type of work completed, the interaction with other supervisees, the quality of the product produced, and the employer's interest in you as a potential candidate.

Rene asked a faculty member generally about his studies of how different personality styles are associated with substance use. The professor invited Rene to sit in on his monthly research team meeting. Rene observed more senior graduate students leading the meeting, discussing their research progress, and generating ideas for studies to be completed by more junior members of the group.

The faculty member remained active and present, but did not direct the group in a "top-down" manner. He encouraged discussion, asked about the status of the projects, and inquired about other studies that might be completed in the future. Rene was taken by the supportive nature of the research team in addition to his interest in the topic of personality assessment and substance use. "Now that is an adviser I could work with!" Rene thought to himself.

Chapter 10

Save the Nobel Prize for Later

> Selecting a research project that requires excessive commitment of time and other resources is best left for later in your professional career.

There is wonderful lore about graduate student researchers who made their initial professional contribution with a study that revolutionized their field. One scientist reportedly wrote his entire dissertation in one page. After his committee got over the shock of such impudence, they discovered the brilliance of the student, who had generated a new equation. Of course it would be desirable to have a research project so amazing that you could ride into your first professional position with notoriety and fame. But, stories such as this one are few and far between.

Typically, influential studies require a huge data set, an atypical study population, rarely used statistics, extensive time commitment, or a lot of money. These factors can be ignored or minimized by faculty members. To this end, a reasonable research project is one that can be completed in a timely manner, with an accessible data set, using existing research methods and analyses.

AVOID OVERLY AMBITIOUS PROJECTS

When we attempt to explain to students the need *not* to undertake an overly involved project, we're reminded of the medical student joke: "What do they call the medical student who graduates last in his class?" The answer is: Doctor! The same logic applies to the question, "What do they call a person who completes a minor dissertation?" Same answer: Doctor!

Remember that the goal of a formal research project, be it a thesis or dissertation, is to satisfy requirements for your advanced degree. As exciting as it would be to influence your field with innovative research, we are actively dissuading you from attempting to be that significant. Although you may well have the ability to perform a wonderfully earth-shaking research project, doing so at this stage of your career is ill-advised. The goal of a dissertation is to contribute to the field while learning the research process. Nowhere is it stated that your dissertation should be published in *Nature* or *Science*.

Our intention to steer you away from an influential project comes from seeing too many graduate students who remain permanently ABD (all but dissertation). The magnitude of some research is so great that it becomes an insurmountable task. Consequently, some students—faced with an awe-inspiring project—find it is easier not to work on it at all.

GUIDELINES FOR THE PRACTICAL DISSERTATION PROJECT

Here are a few simple guidelines that are offered to help you avoid impractical studies:

- Avoid using participants that are difficult to find, such as rare medical disorders, atypical normal individuals (e.g., studies of individuals taller than 6 feet 10 inches), or infrequently co-occurring demographics (e.g., multiracial gay families with children).
- Avoid longitudinal research designs that are "too long." The definition of too long will differ depending on where your participants will be from. However, you should be sensitive to the potential for drop-out if a study requires the participants to return at some point in the future. Of course, monetary incentive for return will always help, but that is no guarantee.
- Avoid studies that require large data sets. Although you might be able to use undergraduate students or members of the community, if your study calls for hundreds of subjects you might be unable to collect all of the information in a timely manner.

THE COUNTERPOSITION

Your adviser, department, or school may disagree with this position. That is because often faculty advisers have a vested interest in your undertaking a complex study. Your adviser likely has a particular research area of interest that comprises studies that have been accomplished by the research team as well as by the adviser alone. Through the completion of a number of smaller studies, a research area is formed and a general contribution is made by the team. When a particular research area gets under the skin of a faculty member, they may forget that a study that might take a few years to conduct would not be the best project to pass along to a graduate student.

EXAMPLES OF IMPRACTICAL STUDIES

Here are a few examples of what might be called "bloated studies" to give you an idea of what may be too big to handle:

- Abby performed a study on substance abuse in outpatient clients across three different psychiatric diagnoses. The disorders were Schizoid Personality Disorder, Schizotypal Personality Disorder, and Undifferentiated Schizophrenia. She worked in an outpatient mental health facility performing psychotherapy. Therefore, she assumed that the task of finding participants and performing the study would be minimized. However, she violated a rule of thumb indicated above; the study included diagnostic categories that are rare.

  When examining a specific population, it is not enough to work in a facility where that specialty population exists. You will need to examine the actual number of individuals that had been seen over a specific time period. In addition, the diagnostic accuracy of those participants should also be assessed before proposing your study. Finally, using a common-sense approach to data collection, you may wish to speak to staff and potential study participants to evaluate their level of interest in participation.

- Chelsea's adviser was well-known in the field for evaluating the effectiveness of different types of psychological therapies. He performed a number of studies and published numerous papers on the pros and cons of different types of treatment programs. Since Chelsea already had an interest in this area of study, she was thrilled when her adviser worked with her to design a research project that would evaluate the efficacy of two different types of psychotherapy in the university's counseling center.

  The study required individuals seeking counseling to sign up for the study, be randomly assigned to one of the two treatment methods, and undergo the 16-week program. The participants would provide information at the outset and then again at the end of treatment regarding their symptoms. Additional post-treatment evaluations were to be performed at one, two, four, and six months following completion of the program.

Although the study was well designed, it was unreasonable for Chelsea for a few reasons, the most important one being that the study was longitudinal. What would Chelsea do if all the members of one treatment group dropped out of therapy? Then there would be no post testing. Consequently, the data from those individuals would not be valid and other participants would have to be located to go through the study. With 25 or 30 subjects in each group, a dropout rate as low as 30 percent would dramatically increase the length of time until the study was completed. Furthermore, the inclusion of additional post-treatment evaluations increases the likelihood of subject dropout.

• Terry's adviser was committed to improving the content and quality of existing intelligence testing. To do so, the test materials would be standardized on a large sample of nonpatient community-dwelling individuals across the adult age span. Terry was offered an opportunity to participate in the standardization of this new test with the added bonus of being able to use the data for his dissertation.

The magnitude of this project necessitated a large standardization sample. His adviser wished to have no fewer than 1,000 participants. It soon became clear that locating, scheduling, and seeing each of these individuals would be horrifically labor intensive for a single individual. In addition, even with the assistance of others, the time required to complete this project would be equally horrendous. So, after six months of literature review and work with his adviser in developing the tasks, Terry saw that he had really signed on to a project that would be better as a first job than as a dissertation.

Despite the resulting tension with his adviser on that project, he dropped the study and wisely went to work on a different project.

Working with an adviser who refuses to consider the reality of the duration of data collection is trouble in waiting. If you do not intend to be a professional student, studies that are designed to be longitudinal or that require multiple pilot studies are best left for your first professional position. In the meantime, entertain studies that sound reasonable to accomplish in a timely manner.

Chapter 11

Concurrent and Absentee Data Collection

The benefit of data collection performed by others or with others must be measured against the accuracy, timing, and personality of those involved.

There are a number of tangible benefits in working with a faculty member who has a coordinated research program. One primary advantage of a research team is that the work is accomplished within a research community, as opposed to working alone. Another benefit is that the data collection phase of a project can be significantly enhanced through either concurrent or absentee data collection. Concurrent data collection refers to working with others to collect data for multiple projects at the same time. Absentee data collection is when others collect your data because you are out of town or do not have access to a subject group.

CONCURRENT DATA COLLECTION

Concurrent data collection occurs when multiple individuals decide to work together to access the same participant sample. This method of collaboration is usually accomplished when a large number of participants is required for a study, the amount of time required by each participant is great, or a sample is difficult to find within specified criteria. A faculty member would be interested in endorsing the concurrent data collection technique because by doing so multiple research projects can be conducted simultaneously.

For instance, one research team found more than 100 individuals with AIDS who agreed to participate in a study of a particular kind of drug that had the potential for reducing physical symptoms of people who were HIV positive. Once a participant was appropriately screened, the chance existed to examine not only the medication but also other questions unrelated to treatment. This provided a great opportunity to incorporate additional studies by conducting companion research examining daily diet, social support, psychological resilience, and other factors regarding these participants.

In other research groups, the exact same data set could be used to answer different research questions. For example, take a study of the mathematical properties of a new personality questionnaire. Usually a large normative sample of hundreds of individuals is required to address the important statistical properties of a new measure. So, once the large volume of participant data is collected, it would be reasonable to address additional research questions about the measure, beyond that answered by a single study. Here are some possible research questions:

• How does this measure compare to other similar measures?
• Is performance on this measure related to major demographic, historical information, or diagnostic information?
• Are scores on this measure consistent over time?
• Are there items that are redundant or unnecessary?

Consequently, by formulating these questions, it would be possible for one study to focus on the factor structure and reliability issues of the research. Another study could then address one of the additional questions proposed above, such as examining the utility of the measure across tasks and individual groupings.

Alternatively, there is convenience in performing two studies at the same time, if the time commitment for the participants allows for this. Winton and Jamal were interested in evaluating the impact of practice on measures typically used in neuropsychological evaluations. The study required college students to perform the same measures every two weeks for a total of four evaluations.

Winton elected to examine measures of intellectual functioning, while Jamal focused on memory tasks. The time that was required for each set of tests was approximately 90 minutes. Jamal and Winton were encouraged to combine the administration of the tasks. In that way, they performed complete three-hour evaluations, each with one-half of the total participants. Then, they shared with each other the appropriate raw data and demographic information obtained for each participant.

The amount of face-to-face time that each student had with participants was the same as it would have been if they had collected all of their own data. However, the process allowed them to use a selected group of participants for two studies, rather than requiring each of the graduate students to find their own sample. This rationale is particularly important when the time commitment for each participant is extensive.

In the case of difficult-to-find participants, joint data collection allows multiple researchers to access multiple sites, leading to greater access to subjects. Another benefit of concurrent data collection relates to the enthusiasm and encouragement that usually occurs when two or more people are working together toward the same goal. Friendly competition to finish scheduling participants can add some positive excitement in completing this phase of a study.

ABSENTEE DATA COLLECTION

Absentee data collection refers to a student's reliance on others to collect the data. Essentially, this method is usually used when you have departed for an internship, or you have moved to some other physical location, and your data are collected by other members of the research team. As with concurrent data collection, researchers coordinate an opportunity to share research participants.

Absentee data collection often occurs when one person has already put in significant time, but has done so without any direct benefit to a specific project. For example, Leslie worked on the development of a questionnaire that would gather pertinent information about attitudes of immigrant drug users. However, this test required multiple revisions and considerable data collection to move it to a state where it became a usable form. Hani was responsible for the setup and calibration of technical equipment in a professor's laboratory. Both Hani and Leslie were parts of research teams, and their work on the front end was helpful to everyone else who would be using the questionnaire that Leslie helped develop and the equipment in the laboratory that Hani helped set up. These students made a contribution although they did not directly collect any data.

Jerry was a head research assistant to more junior graduate students prior to leaving town for a one-year internship in another state. In his role as head of the research assistants, he trained the more junior students in how the studies were to be run and how participants go through the process. But, as often can occur, while he was working as a research assistant his own work was not getting completed.

With an eye toward absentee data collection, he went to the faculty adviser of the research team. He proposed that the now trained students perform
Jerry's data collection and he would return every few months to monitor the
progress. He had funding to pay the students who would then be his own
research assistants, if they agreed. All of those involved felt confident with
regard to the administration of the study, accuracy of the data, and fairness of
payment.

The adviser may similarly be in favor of others collecting data for your
project if, for instance, you provided significant time and effort in setting up
the laboratory equipment. What may be deemed an acceptable contribution
of hands-on time will be at the discretion of the faculty member, but certainly
you would need to clarify with the department and the adviser that such a tit-
for-tat arrangement could be made.

PITFALLS OF CONCURRENT DATA COLLECTION

Potential flaws of concurrent data collection pertain mostly with how well
you can work with another person—and how well they can work with you. If
it turns out that the other researcher is not adhering to agreed on procedures
or otherwise is not consistent with your administration method, their data
become unusable.

The problem with the other researcher might not even be intentional.
There really are people out there who are not as competent as you when it
comes to sticking to standardized procedures. You need to find out ahead of
time how competent your fellow researcher is. The last thing you need is to
spend months worrying about the competence of others when your research
project and dissertation is at stake.

What about timing? No one will be as motivated to finish as you are. You
might have a data collection partner who wants to wait until the following
semester to propose or wants to wait until the next academic year before
beginning data collection. At that point, your project may likewise be pushed
back even if you are ready to begin.

On the other hand, you might be the one who needs more time. Although
the other person is ready to begin data collection, you may not yet feel that
your project is ready to propose. Consequently, you might select a project of
convenience that is not of interest to you, or you might propose your study
prematurely. In the former case, your motivation may fade after your data are
collected. In the latter example, your jumping the gun to propose might result
in a poorly designed study that is rejected by your committee, forcing you to
begin again altogether.

Obviously, if someone else is collecting your data, as is the case with absentee collection, these pragmatic concerns are no longer an issue at all. You will be put in the position of being able to monitor from afar, without needing to micromanage the process. When a procedural snag occurs, working with a colleague will also give you a chance to resolve it with someone who knows the issues as well as you. Any difficulties with the protocol would then be brought to your adviser, with some mutually agreed on solutions.

PITFALLS OF ABSENTEE DATA COLLECTION

One can easily be tempted to do a study in which the data will be collected by someone else. In fact, you will probably be told that by doing so, your project will be a piece of cake because someone else will be doing all of the time-consuming work. Your committee chair might even tempt you by saying that if you choose to go on your internship out of town, by the time you return the data collection will be completed.

As exciting as this prospect might be, it is important to become aware of potential pitfalls so that you can decide if this *sure thing* is too good to be true. First, evaluate what your next step would be if the data are not collected. Imagine if one year from now, when you return from your internship, you find that no subjects have been run, the laboratory is in disrepair, or the person you thought was going to collect data decided not to do so. At that time, you will have no recourse. As well intentioned as your committee chair and research group colleagues might have been, with no data collected you will either need a new project or tackle data collection yourself.

In addition to the irritation of the data not being collected one year after leaving your school, motivation for working on this will likely have waned as well. If you remained vigilant in monitoring the study from afar, the lack of data should not come as a surprise. Nevertheless, your time on internship waiting for participants to be seen would make for a year with a constant nagging feeling about your dissertation. That nagging feeling comes from not only the normal worry experienced by others but also an additional feeling of having no control over your own project. After a break from your project, the energy required to become actively involved is greater than had you been working on it over the course of the year.

Now, let us assume that the data were actually collected by a research team, a hired graduate student, or by your best friend. Your absentee supervision may result in nonstandardized administration procedures, omitted information, inaccurate documentation, or any number of problems that would result in erroneous data. If you find after the fact that your data are inaccurate, you will really be in trouble—with the only potential solution being to collect the data again with a new sample.

WHEN EITHER METHOD WORKS THERE ARE BENEFITS

Both absentee and concurrent data collection offer great benefits for the graduate student researcher. With concurrent collection, the struggles involving finding, scheduling, and processing the participants are shared with another, reducing the amount of time and effort you will need to devout to those aspects of a project.

When it works, having others collect some or all of your data can be a tremendous help in moving through your research project. However, when deciding to go in this direction, you should be aware of the potential conflict of working with others who may not be as competent, timely, accurate, or committed as you might be.

Chapter 12

Archival Data Collection

The ease of using preexisting data must be measured against their inflexibility, credibility, and simplicity in preparing for statistical analysis.

Imagine this scenario: You're minding your own business on a beautiful spring day, one of the first warm spring days of the year. So, you're driving down a main street with your car windows open. As you slow down to stop at a red light, a black cargo van pulls up on the left side of your car. As you look over at the van, the front seat passenger leans out of his window and says, "Hey pal! Are you interested in buying an iPad with an awesome sound system very cheap?"

Before you can respond, he points to a bank parking lot to your right. "Pull in there," he says. "You can check out the system and then take cash out of the ATM while we put it in your car."

There is no way the guys in the van can possibly know you're a poor graduate student who would love to have an iPad III with Bluetooth wireless speaker stereo system. In fact, you've been a regular "window shopper" at the Apple Store for a number of months. But, your credit card is nearly maxed out, and there is no way that your parents would count this as a necessity. You had decided that until you get your job after you finish your dissertation, you'll use your computer that's a few years old . . . and played through the same crummy speakers you've had all along.

But, here is someone who would easily sell you a premier system and at a price you could afford. How convenient! One-stop shopping and all you have to do is pull over. You could have that first-class stereo system at home within minutes—all for the cost of a budget model.

As tempting as the offer is, by the time the light turns red, you decide the risk isn't worth it. You mumble "no thanks" and drive on.

Although this might sound more like a bad movie scenario than real life, you may have an opportunity in your academic setting to have a similar experience. The potential pros and cons related to archival data collection are similar to those in that scene.

ARCHIVAL DATA

Let's first get some perspective relating to the use of preexisting data for an academic research project. At a basic level, data are considered archival if the researcher is not the one who has collected the information. Many schools require that you perform your own data collection in an effort to fully appreciate the research process. The rationale is that if you ever need to learn the processes required for face-to-face data collection, it is better to do so while still in the cocoon of an academic community rather than after you have left that protective environment.

However, some programs will allow research to be performed with information that has already been gathered by others. These studies are usually approved if the student can demonstrate that the existing data are sufficiently interesting and meaningful to answer a research question. Any method of gathering data that have already been collected is considered archival data collection. Archival data could come in the form of additional or supplemental information from a study that had already been completed. Or, a hospital or organization might have been collecting data for years and it is sitting there waiting for a student to use it.

Often, academics will focus on one particular question in a research study, later returning to the data to see if other research questions can be answered. It is also possible that data might have been collected in a study, but the investigator never had time to analyze them. Consequently, they will sometimes gift the data to a graduate student as a study, provided they are actively involved in the project.

Alternatively, consider a clinical setting where you might have worked as a practicum student or as an intern. You may become interested in a research question that could be answered by evaluating the existing records at that facility. For example, you might analyze length of hospitalization stay across diagnostic categories, level of intellectual functioning relative to demographic background, or comparability and accuracy of different measures of emotional functioning. Any of these examples demonstrate the variety of opportunities that might exist from tapping into data that already have been collected.

What benefits might you enjoy from retrospective data collection? Just as when being offered the latest computer equipment and sound system, the exciting benefits will pop into your mind faster than you can clap your hands together in glee. Although the advantages may seem obvious, here are a few to consider:

1. **No data collection frustrations.** Previously collected data eliminates all of the hassles entailed in the data collection phase of the study. More to the point, consider the time saved when you will not be required to locate participants, evaluate their appropriateness, schedule appointments, and administer whatever procedures may be required for your study.

2. **Limited new learning required.** There is no need for you to obtain training yourself or to teach others new techniques, administration guidelines, or scoring procedures.

3. **No piloting new techniques or measures.** When collecting your own data with a new interview form, questionnaire, or test measure, you will likely need to pilot the instrument on a sample to make sure that it works correctly before even getting to the point of collecting data to answer your research question. Using archival data eliminates the aggravation of piloting a new procedure or instrument.

4. **Accessibility of data.** Moving away from arguments that focus on the convenience of existing data, archival information can be used to address research questions in cases when doing one's own data collection becomes unreasonable. For example, studies evaluating rare occurrences or using large numbers of participants might not otherwise be accomplished without preexisting data being available.

Barb's master's thesis assessed patients in a rehabilitation center less than one month following a stroke. Although a great idea in theory, as the facility admitted approximately eight patients per month, data collection of only 32 patients took over 18 months. The delay was because most of the subjects failed to meet inclusion criteria of the study. If Barb had been given the opportunity to evaluate data already collected from stroke patients, she would have jumped at the chance in a heartbeat.

Taken together, there are at least four—and probably more—advantages in making use of existing data that have already been collected.

That's the good news; now for the bad news. The cautions relating to archived data are actually quite similar to the concerns raised about the iPad being sold by two suspicious-looking guys out of the back of a cargo van. Sure it is convenient, but what potential problems come to mind?

1. **There's no guarantee that the product is of the high quality claimed**. A database that is generated by a clinical setting, for instance, is subject to the variability among those who contributed. Although clinicians would like to assume that all individuals working in their clinic gather information accurately, the potential inaccuracy needs to be considered.

2. **You do not know where the product came from**. Along similar lines as above, the actual source of the data needs to be assessed. Were the data collected by the faculty member or by previous graduate students? If collected by students, do you know who they are and if the quality of their data is trustworthy for accuracy? Even if you trust the data, there may be others who do not.

Charles wanted to do his research using archival data from a previous study. However, as it turned out, the original researchers had never obtained appropriate approval from the university's Investigational Review Board. Without confirmation of informed consent or adherence to any other required elements of a study, Charles was essentially asking to perform additional analyses on data that were illegitimately collected and, thus, unacceptable by any standards.

3. **Customer service may be lacking**. When working with something offered by only one person, you are locked in to dealing with that individual for the long term. For a stereo, the issue might be replacing a faulty component. Regarding a research project, the concerns include any difficulties relating to theoretical, statistical, writing, or personality differences that stymie the ability to accomplish the project.

That's not to say that the owner of the data is necessarily wrong. The data belong to that individual, who is therefore entitled to make whatever requests deemed necessary to extract relevant information. Unfortunately, the graduate student is then put in the uncomfortable position of performing work that may not be of interest.

4. **A ready-made system lacks flexibility**. With archival data, you can make no additions, only deletions. Your review of the literature relating to your project could demand that an additional measure—or that a newer measure—be included. Similarly, your committee may believe that for every subject in your study you need to have an IQ score, the parents' occupation, the subject's high school grade point average, or the date of the last hospitalization.

Likewise, you may be unable to determine if data collected were done in the same order and under the same conditions for all subjects. Alternatively, if the order of test administration affects performance, the order might not have been counterbalanced during collection. If any of these problems are relevant, then you are potentially going to do a study that will at best not be a valid contribution to the field, but at worst might be unable to answer your study questions.

5. **Noncompliant format**. If your stereo plays compact discs, but all you have at home is MP3, then you will have to reformat all of your information. Although not impossible, the time and effort required to reformat the material may not justify its use. Existing data can be available in an electronic format, data sheets, transcribed information, or raw videotapes. Electronical-

ly analyzing data already in an appropriate file is certainly easier than becoming involved in a project that would require transcription of videotapes before the information could be used.

Despite all of the concerns presented above, there is nothing that is intrinsically wrong with archival research. However, you may recognize the hesitancy in supporting this type of research wholeheartedly. The benefits of using collected data must be weighed against the potential challenges that can also occur. If the topic that you are studying necessitates using preexisting data (i.e., requiring atypical patient samples or large numbers of participants), then you will need to accept the possibility that the specific questions you have will be constrained by the data that exist.

Archival data present the challenge of satisfying the institution that is keeping the data, while at the same time satisfying the requirements for a research project of the department. Clarify with potential faculty who may serve on your committee that information may alter their interest in the study as well as potential changes they may have for the study design. You will need to evaluate the viability of a study using existing data against each of the hazards that are mentioned above. Being forewarned is being forearmed!

Chapter 13

Maximizing Flexibility

Be prepared to revise or replace your study if one idea does not seem to be working.

The *American Heritage Dictionary* defines the adjective "dynamic" as characterized by "continuous change, activity, or progress." The greatest success in completing a dissertation is found in individuals who adopt a view of the process as being dynamic.

Linear thinking must end. It is time to resist the inclination to assume that the idea you first decided on will be the project you will end up with. Think of the process as one in which a person takes a canoe from one point to another point. Your direction and mode of travel will generally be the same. Your goal in reaching the final destination will also be unchanged. However, the exact path will vary depending on what obstacles arise in your travels. You must continuously evaluate what is directly in front of you, as well as what challenges might occur "downstream." Once the complications are identified, you change what you are doing in order to achieve your goal of completing your research project.

Consider the scenarios below that may better explain our position about viewing the entire process dynamically. These real-life situations demonstrate the low, medium, and high levels of dynamic thinking that are often observed with graduate students working on their dissertations.

THE STORY OF MIKE

Mike was in his fourth year of graduate school. He had worked with a faculty member for his master's thesis and decided to continue to work with the same faculty member for his dissertation. The project required pilot data testing to ensure the viability of the apparatuses, instrumentation, and procedures.

Excited to begin the process, Mike ran the number of subjects (40 in all) required by his adviser for the pilot study. He then followed the instructions of his adviser and wrote a formal summary of the data. The document was read, edited, and returned. Mike corrected the document and presented the revision to his adviser. The adviser promptly reread it, made additional changes, and returned it for further corrections. After a number of additional drafts were circulated, Mike's adviser gave him permission to use the pilot data in the proposal for the full research project.

Mike's dissertation prospectus suffered the same fate of "revise and resubmit" as did his pilot data. After 11 proposal drafts, more than three years had passed. The adviser changed the project a number of times, required information to be added that was removed a few revisions later, and became less and less encouraging about the study.

A friend asked Mike the important question: "Why are you working with that adviser?" His response was clear and coherent. He stated that his adviser had worked on the literature review for over three years, was quite familiar with the topic, already collected and analyzed pilot data, and Mike could see that the adviser was soon going to allow him to propose the dissertation project.

Savvy readers of this scenario will see the writing on the wall. You are shouting from your chairs "Bail out before it is too late!" You see the potential proof to the adage that the best predictor of future behavior is past behavior. That is exactly what truly came to pass. Data collection took less than one year and required no contact with the adviser. However, when the data analyses resulted in findings that went against the hypotheses proposed by the adviser, the adviser required the analyses to be rerun.

Although the findings turned out to be the same, the write up was equally painful. Draft after draft of the dissertation manuscript were sent back and forth over two years. No interpretation of the data was ever fully satisfactory to this adviser. In the end, Mike's rigidity in sticking to the same project with the same adviser resulted in years of frustration. Had he elected to work with a different subject matter, or an entirely different adviser, he might have been able to complete a dissertation in significantly less time than the six years it ended up taking him.

THE STORY OF LILA

Lila was a practicum student at a hospital. Through her experiences there, she generated a research question relating to predicting success in mental health treatment based on data that were obtained in the initial intake interview. She worked with an adviser who approved the concept of an archival study from the psychology records at the facility where Lila was working. Her adviser recommended that before going through a formal dissertation proposal, she should get approval from the hospital. This was because Lila's adviser wanted to be sure that the study would be successful before she put too much work into it.

Informal discussions with one of the psychologists at the hospital were quite promising; he was supportive of the study. Lila was told to send a letter to the head of psychology at the hospital, requesting access to intake information and treatment outcome data. Four months went by and Lila had not received a response to her letter. She did not want to be too pushy, so she thought that she would merely wait until she obtained a response.

At the suggestion of her adviser, Lila called the head of psychology at the hospital where the request was sent. She was told that he had forgotten and would get back to her in six to eight weeks with a final decision about her access to the mental health documents. Over the course of the following two months, Lila's adviser encouraged her to seek out other facilities where archival intake interview data could be collected. (At the same time, Lila was considering other studies altogether.)

When the phone call arrived a few weeks later, the psychologist of the initial facility told her that he was opposed to her using the data. Regardless of the reason for his refusal, Lila had already found two other sites where the responsible staff not only encouraged the study but also wished to be on her dissertation committee.

Although the project was generated by her work at one facility, she was able to generalize that information and apply it to a new setting. So, after a slow and passive beginning, Lila made use of a dynamic process by seeking out other facilities where the study could be conducted.

THE STORY OF SCOTT

Scott knew that he needed to become involved in a research project that would be of a relatively short duration. He also knew that he wanted to do a study that would serve as a contribution, even if it were a modest contribution. So, Scott spoke with physicians at the hospital where he was on practicum. He discovered that there was one physician who was interested in examining the psychological aspects of specific medical ailments.

Scott did his work and reviewed the relevant studies. He worked diligently, on an almost daily basis, reading, writing, and learning this new area of study. A dissertation committee was formed. Scott successfully defended his dissertation proposal, which gave him a mandate to begin data collection.

Unfortunately, soon after beginning data collection he realized that the medical conditions he was seeking to find were quite rare. The limited prevalence of the disorder certainly made the study of its psychological implication a worthy study, but NOT for a dissertation. Scott estimated that he would be able to evaluate two patients per month, a yield that would take over two years to generate the 50 participants that he needed for his study.

Within two months of coming to a clear realization of the potential length of time of data collection, Scott had dropped his study. He presented the issues to his adviser. Scott successfully requested that the study be scrapped, evaluated a different topic area, generated a new proposal, and formally proposed the new project approximately six months after his first study was proposed.

One year later, his dissertation was defended. By learning a new area and writing a new proposal Scott had taken an additional six months to begin his data collection. However, he nonetheless had formally defended his dissertation more than six months before his data collection would have ended for his initial project. One could point out that Scott's weakness was his lack of knowledge regarding the prevalence of the disorder in the first study. Be that as it may, he expertly demonstrated an ability to shift to a new project when a previous one seemed too time intensive.

RESEARCH PROJECTS CAN BE DERAILED FOR VARIOUS REASONS

There's an old adage that says that nothing is certain except death and taxes. This means that the only two things that are unavoidable are death and taxes. Where research is concerned, however, there are no unavoidable difficulties. A research project can be derailed by endless stalling, failed data collection, inappropriate additions made by advisers or supervisors, or any other of a myriad of problems.

Regardless of who is to blame for the disruptions that you experience, when all is said and done, you are the one who is ultimately responsible. The argument that you "have spent six months writing a proposal" will not seem meaningful when you are still collecting data five years later. *You* are the one who requires the completion of the study to achieve your degree. *You* are the one who will be working in a position that is beneath your expertise because you will not have your degree. *You* are the one who will be ABD if you choose to wait passively rather than act assertively.

Resist traveling in a straight line. Now is the time to approach your research project dynamically. Take the project into your own hands, find the best path, and be prepared to change it if those changes will better serve you to reach the goal of completing your study.

Chapter 14

Locale and Availability of Data Collection

The locale and availability of your data source will make a difference in terms of expenses and time if changes or additions have to be made.

As noted in a previous chapter when concurrent, collaborative, and archival data collection were discussed, there can certainly be difficulties in relying on the work of others for your dissertation. Consequently, most neophyte researchers collect their own data.

YOUR DATA SHOULD BE AVAILABLE LOCALLY

The goal should be to find a sample that can be collected locally. That is, you want to avoid having participants in your research a long distance from where you live. As a corollary, a research study must access study samples that are of sufficient availability. Choosing a patient population that is rare and unique might be fascinating; however, this is only feasible if there is evidence that this rare group can provide enough subjects to warrant study. This might be easy to figure out simply by speaking to individuals who have access to such a sample. But many researchers do not take this simple step before beginning a proposal.

CAN YOU FIND ENOUGH SUBJECTS?

This should be the first question you ask yourself: Can I find enough subjects who are locally available and that I can easily locate to conduct a research project which can be finished in a reasonable amount of time?

Patty, a student in a graduate dental program, was fascinated by kratom, which comes from the leaves of a tree grown in Southeast Asia. The leaves are chewed for medicinal purposes. Although kratom is a controlled substance in some countries, such as Thailand and Sweden, it is still legal in the United States. Some Southeast Asian immigrants who may use this substance may not know this. Kratom is most often used by people from Thailand or other Southeast Asian countries—people who come to the urban clinic where Patty was doing a residency. Patty wanted to study whether the users of kratom were aware of detrimental oral effects and whether there would be more plaque buildup or periodontal disease among kratom users versus non-users.

Although the Institutional Review Board at her college had concerns about legal protection for study subjects who admitted to kratom usage, the members of the IRB did not know whether she could find enough admitted users of kratom. As it turned out, Patty had difficulty finding subjects who would agree to sign a form to be part of the study because they were fearful of legal sanctions. After 18 months of soliciting subjects, Patty was still far short of the number of subjects she needed. Her adviser suggested she travel to other urban areas—some hundreds of miles away—to find dentists who might have possible kratom users that she could include in her research.

Devon was visiting an aunt and uncle in Chile when an earthquake occurred. He volunteered to help in rescue operations. However, it was working as part of a rescue team that he encountered children who were seriously affected by the earthquake and he started thinking about doing a study on the psychological effects on children after surviving an earthquake.

Devon extended his stay by a few weeks to begin collecting data and then came home to write a proposal for his dissertation on this subject. As he presented his ideas to his adviser and then his committee, it was suggested that he gather additional information generated by the initial set of interviews, requiring follow-up discussions with his participants. He was also asked to include more subjects than those he initially saw. Altogether, before his data were collected, Devon returned three additional times to Chile in order to meet the demands of the study.

Michele had a seemingly straightforward project in which she was to evaluate only 30 individuals referred for counseling at a nearby psychology clinic. The idea was to see all individuals who had experienced physical abuse at the hand of their spouse. Knowing that the clinic was somewhat busy, she felt confident that she would be able to accrue the required sample pool of 30 participants in short order.

Thirty participants certainly seemed like a small number. But, it became a rather large number when patients referred for counseling were informed of the study. Every new client was told of the research project, that it would require completing a single 30-minute questionnaire. However, only seven of the new clients to the clinic enrolled in the study after six months of data collection. Either the incidence of abuse or the *report* of abuse was much smaller than initially theorized by Michele and her committee. At that rate of data collection, Michele likely required another 18 months in order to get close to completing gathering questionnaires from what was initially thought to be a rather easy sample.

GATHER INFORMATION BEFORE COMMITTING TO A RESEARCH PROJECT

All three researchers had great ideas for their research projects. However, Patty didn't realize before starting her research how difficult it would be sign up study participants. Devon never considered that he would have to travel back to Chile in order to complete his project. Michele failed to consider actual participation rates from a group that she thought was readily accessible.

In all instances, by gathering more information from others prior to their personal commitment to pursue their research topic, they might have saved both time and money by finding subjects who would be closer to home and more readily available. Therefore, prior to studying rare entities or difficult-to-find populations you will need to evaluate whether data can be collected in a reasonable period of time.

BE AWARE OF MURPHY'S LAW

Be realistic about the availability of research participants and about possible complications. It's better to proceed when planning a dissertation research project with Murphy's Law in mind. Murphy's Law is an adage that quite simply states: If anything can go wrong, it will go wrong.

Therefore, in planning a research project, look at what could go wrong. In particular, consider whether you can get enough subjects, whether you could encounter additional expenses, or whether you could be delayed in data collection by strange or bizarre occurrences. As Patty, Devon, and Michele can attest, if anything could go wrong, it probably will. It might be better to choose a study with fewer risks than be caught in the vortex of Murphy's Law.

Chapter 15

The Financial Pain of Research

There are almost always hidden costs that you never expected in the beginning when planning your research project.

When mulling over the potential research possibilities that exist for you, an additional item of consideration is the projected cost of the study. The cost of time and potential delays in completing your project are discussed in a number of places in this book. But what about real costs? As in, how much money will you need to complete your study?

CONSIDER ALL POTENTIAL COSTS

In most cases, the actual cost is minimal. But do not be fooled by the committee chair who informs you that the cost "shouldn't be too much." There are some test materials that are copyrighted and are required to be purchased. Don't begin your professional career by gaining access to materials by violating legal and ethical guidelines.

Materials can include the one-time-only cost of test kits, data analysis or other software, and supplies to create test stimuli. Ongoing "consumables" can include test forms or the individual scoring of test protocols on measures that require it. If payment for participation in the study is to be made, then that cost needs to be considered as well.

Steve had a research study in which the ability to smell accurately was compared across two groups of 30 individuals. In order to complete the study, performance on a specific olfactory test was used as the measure. The tasks had to be given to all 60 participants in the project. After being hit with a $30 per protocol cost for the smell test, Steve was then told that it cost an additional $30 per test to score the findings as a measure of personality. He quickly tabulated that it would cost him at least $3,600 to do his study, assuming that he would not have to throw out any of the data.

Lily was grateful to her committee chair who offered to buy required computer software for her to perform her research project. However, neither Lily nor her supervisor realized what additional hardware requirements were needed in terms of video cards, audio cards, and computer processing speed. Although the expensive software was purchased for her, in order to use it effectively Lily was forced to purchase hundreds of dollars of computer upgrades.

TIME AND TRAVEL EXPENSES

Don't neglect travel time and expenses. When Devon had to return to Chile three times to gather additional information and do follow ups with his subjects, he had the expense of round-trip airplane tickets, lodging, food, and incidental expenses. When Patty had to go to other cities to find additional subjects, she had to travel by car, stay in motels and hotels, and sometimes use taxi cabs to efficiently get to appointments with other dentists. These kinds of costs can add hundreds or thousands of dollars to any other costs encountered in a research project.

PAYING PARTICIPANTS

Sometimes in order to attract people to be part of a research project, a stipend or payment is offered. It may not be much per subject, but for a graduate student any additional expenses can be burdensome.

In order to study women with depression, Clarisa was advised by her dissertation committee that she should pay each subject not only for their time but also for travel expenses. Clarisa, as a struggling graduate student, did not see how she could afford to offer these kinds of incentives to study participants. She considered a grant and spent several months writing a grant proposal and waiting for responses from funding agencies.

HOW TO CUT PERSONAL EXPENSES

Are there some answers to defraying these costs? Sure there are. Some answers may seem obvious, but think creatively to find what works best for you. Consider concurrent data collection (see Chapter 11) as one way to reduce costs. If you and another researcher share the cost of payments to participants, then by working together, you could cut your cost in half.

Sometimes individuals are less interested in actually receiving money for participating in a study. Instead, they may be happier donating their money to a charity of their choice. In doing so, it is the good will you will achieve with the participant that will be more motivating to them than actually getting a check. In addition, if you are giving $10 for two hours of participation, no one is going to sign up in hopes of getting rich. Yet, they may certainly do so in hopes that it will benefit their charitable organization.

Once you get a well-motivated participant, they might even be interested in recruiting others to their study. What better recruitment tool than a participant going to others and saying, "If you qualify for the research project that is being done, the program will give $10 to our organization."

Although it is obvious to experienced researchers, those early in their careers don't realize that there are potential funding opportunities available for research projects. Interested in medical conditions? Consider approaching large national organizations, such as whatever would be comparable to the American Cancer Society or American Heart Association for the condition you are studying. Or see if local, rather than national, offices of the larger organizations have funding opportunities.

And do not think that any one condition has only one organization studying its properties. For example, Parkinson's disease is being studied by organizations including the Parkinson's Disease Foundation, American Parkinson Disease Association, National Parkinson Foundation, and the Michael J. Fox Foundation for Parkinson's Research. There are often ways to seek modest sums from a few different organizations, provided the studies are acceptable to all players.

Organizations unrelated to your field of interest might also have funds available. Whether it's a company donating a product to test it in the field, approaching your own graduate school for a few hundred dollars of supplies, or getting financial backing from a local organization that provides funding for any type of professional research, opportunities for monies exist.

When looking for ways to get external funding, also think about using multiple sources. Six donations of $250 each might be easier to acquire than a single donation from one company for $1,500.

But, just like trying to get your study off of the ground, seeking funding will require interest, research, and perseverance by you!

BE AWARE OF THE POTENTIAL EXPENSES

Don't begin a research project without being fully aware of all the potential costs and expenses. There are enough stresses for graduate students without adding additional financial stresses.

Part IV

Selecting Your Committee

Chapter 16

Selecting Your Adviser

> Your strongest professional source of knowledge and support is your adviser.
> Choose wisely.

When you are finished with your education, you will be granted your degree.
Of course you will have earned it by doing much of the work. But, you also
understand that you will have had assistance along the way. Yes, your dissertation is your project. But, the best way to get through the process is to have
someone help you throughout the ordeal.

YOUR ADVISER PLAYS A KEY ROLE

Your responsibility is to manage the project, but you need an adviser to serve
as the needed resource, facilitator, guide, mentor, and advocate over the
course of this endeavor. Your adviser, who will also be the chairperson of
your research committee, will be the primary contact person for you throughout the study and the writing of the dissertation. The chair of your research
committee should be someone who will navigate the delicate balancing act of
serving as liaison between the university, committee members, and you—the
student.

The role of the chair can be of particular importance if you find yourself
in a problematic situation. Your data site is no longer available? Check with
the committee chair to work together on a solution. You need funding to
finance your project? See what suggestions are offered by your chair. Data
collection assistance is required to complete the study on time? See if the
chair has other students who can help with various aspects of the project.

Require assistance with interpreting your statistics . . . or in writing your dissertation draft? You got it—the chair will be your primary contact and first "go to" source of information in all of these areas.

SELECT CRITERIA FOR YOUR ADVISER

Therefore, you will need to carefully study your adviser possibilities along a number of professional and personal criteria. Professionally, this individual will serve as your resource for expertise in the area of study. If you cannot find a faculty member who is an expert in the particular area you want to study, then try to find a potential adviser who is competent in a similar research area with sufficient knowledge in your interest area to make the transition an appropriate one.

From a personal perspective, your committee chair need not be your pal. However, your adviser should be an individual whose work style, accessibility, and comradeship will see you through a difficult, long, and perhaps arduous process. If you can, find an adviser with whom you can speak openly and freely about your project and the various obstacles you encounter.

Informal discussions with current students and graduated advisees of a faculty member will provide important information as to the success or failure of that professional as a chair. But it's even better if you have had a relationship with your potential adviser prior to asking that person to head up your committee.

For instance, Samantha had an assistantship with her primary adviser and already had a working relationship with her. So, Samantha knew many things about this faculty person ahead of time.

"I knew she was organized, had a great working knowledge of statistics, was calm, thoughtful, and encouraging," Samantha said. "Another thing I liked about her was that she fostered my independence. That was important to me."

But Samantha found that her adviser had some weaknesses. For instance, she was not a clinician. However, Samantha later said that this worked out fine. "I selected other committee members who provided the kind of balance I wanted between academics and clinical faculty." Samantha had a distinct advantage in having worked on other projects with her adviser. She knew what to expect of her committee chair.

Unfortunately, Derek did not have a favorable outcome in finding a strong adviser. He had not worked with his adviser in the past as many students have done—often as an assistant in the faculty member's research lab, for instance. However, once Derek began working on his own research, it became clear that they had different expectations as to what each one wished for their relationship.

Derek would find that he and his adviser did not agree about the direction of the research proposal. When issues were raised by Derek, he was instructed to "go to the literature," studying existing papers and formally writing a summary at his adviser's request. It became clear that these exercises were used less as a learning experience and more as punishment for disagreeing with the adviser.

It was obvious to both Derek and his adviser that they should have talked more about their expectations for each other prior to the commitment each had made. Moreover, discussions had not taken place about what to do if results did not go in the direction proposed by the adviser.

Just because Samantha found an adviser she could work with, that doesn't mean that she would be without conflict. Separate and apart from having a good working relationship with an adviser, there are other practical matters that should be addressed in a clear and direct manner. In brief, these other practical matters revolve around these questions:

- Will the adviser have the interest and availability to work with you?
- Does this person have enough time to take on this project?
- Is she interested in your research?
- Does he have skills that you haven't yet learned or are in the process of learning? In other words, will he be an asset to your learning new skills?
- Does she have experience in being an adviser?
- Is he planning to take a sabbatical during the time you will be in the middle of your project?
- Is she considering relocating to another college? If she leaves, what accommodations will be made for existing students?

Although asking these questions might be uncomfortable, by not doing so you are opening yourself up to potential frustrations down the road when one of these possible issues surfaces.

Chapter 17

Selecting Other Committee Members (Part I) . . . Choose Whom You Know

Choose committee members you know and with whom you know you can work.

One of the most positive aspects of the dissertation process is being able to work with professionals with whom you have already learned. For instance, your committee could comprise former teachers and supervisors who are ready to assist you in making the transition from student to colleague.

What a great feeling it is to be able to know the personalities of your committee members before entering the room for a meeting about your proposal or when you are defending your proposal. Furthermore, there is no doubt that your comfort level will improve when you look around the table at individuals who have all been supportive of your education thus far.

The chances are significantly reduced that you will not be blindsided in the process of preparing your proposal and then later defending it if you have professionals on your committee with whom you have worked and whom you know. The last thing you need in planning your research, carrying out your project, or preparing your dissertation is someone on your committee creating chaos with a new criticism at the eleventh hour or during your actual defense.

WHICH FACULTY MEMBERS DO YOU KNOW BEST?

Who are the faculty members who know you best? Who are the instructors you enjoy spending time talking to, both in terms of technical information as well as when not talking about professional issues?

Crystal enjoyed her research and technical writing professor so much, that she made use of his office hours on a regular basis. Aside from discussing issues relating to information provided in the classroom, Crystal and her professor moved discussions into other areas of study. The professor found Crystal insightful and with an excellent sense of research beyond what was taught in the classroom. The professor worked with her in seeking some consultation in reviewing articles for journals, discussion of research ideas, and even asking Crystal to serve as a coauthor on a manuscript written by the professor.

Clearly, both Crystal and the professor benefited mutually from their professional interactions. When it came time to begin considering a research project, it took no great thinking for Crystal to put the research and technical writing professor at the top of her list of faculty to serve on her committee. Although the research topic was not within the area that would have made that professor appropriate to chair, Crystal's familiarity with the faculty member made the choice easy to include on the committee.

CHOOSE PEOPLE YOU KNOW WELL

Therefore, when deciding who you would like on your committee, consider people you know. For example, you could make a list of about six people you would like to initially ask to be part of your advisory committee from these categories:

- Past or present professors and instructors
- Past or present colleagues you have worked with in an internship
- Past or present people who are in your field with whom you have worked
- Friends and acquaintances who know something about your field of study

If there are any candidates for your advisory committee on your list that you do not know well, you should talk to other students to find out more about these people, discover if they have been on another students' advisory committee, and try to make sure they are going to be compatible with your research and dissertation ideas.

It is important to make sure you choose a committee who can share your vision for your project. That may involve spending some time in the beginning explaining your vision and getting their honest feedback.

CHOOSE PEOPLE WHO MAY WORK WELL TOGETHER

It is also important to try to ensure that they will be compatible with one another. Jacqueline found her experience working with her committee very frustrating. "I thought the committee members I selected would work well with each other," Jacqueline said, "but I was wrong. There were personality conflicts and, in addition, I was getting contradictory instructions by different committee members. I felt at times like I was running around in circles."

Jujuan, after working with his committee for a few months, began to feel that requests for edits were politically motivated. Beyond that, he also suspected that at least one committee member was biased against him. While Jujuan did not want to think that a professor he respected would be biased because of his race, this committee member kept insisting Jujuan's proposal was not right and did not agree with others on the committee about the quality of Jujuan's writing and about the adequacy of the research design.

CHOOSE PEOPLE WHO UNDERSTAND YOUR GOALS

Ideally, it is wonderful when all committee members have the student's ultimate career goals in mind, particularly when there is discussion and recommendations about what topics, methods, and even what publications should be sought out (much later) for publication of the dissertation.

Casandra felt she was lucky in regard to the composition of her committee. "I saw each one of my committee members as understanding my research goals," she said, "and they all seemed to want to advance my learning and ultimately finishing my dissertation."

Casandra also said that she felt grateful to each of her committee members because she knew she could work with them. "I needed and wanted a committee that was prompt, deadline-oriented, and practical. They helped me stick to the task and get the dissertation done in a timely manner."

Chapter 18

Selecting Other Committee Members (Part II) . . . Know Whom You Choose

> If you have the wrong people on your committee, it can delay your progress
> and ultimately your graduation.

The ability to call all of your committee members by their first name is not synonymous with "smooth sailing" as you make your way over all of the hurdles. People are people, and they do not necessarily get along with each other or come to the table with the same level of commitment to the project.

Can a committee member be too nice? Ask Aaron, who loved his committee chair. "He was so affable and agreeable with everything I did," Aaron recalls, "that I thought this whole dissertation project would move along wonderfully well. How could it not? We got along so well and he was always complimentary of my work in his classes."

However, once the proposal was complete after a year of work, Aaron was shocked when his committee rejected his proposal outright. "Yes, he was pleasant and agreeable," Aaron says, "but he was also very lenient and let me do things that the committee just couldn't accept."

Aaron was sent back to the drawing board and, fortunately, worked with a less permissive committee chair. The new chair was more critical and guided Aaron to finish a proposal that his committee approved. The former chair remained on the committee, as he remained supportive of Aaron's work. But, it was clear that the rest of the committee was more appropriately critical than the first chair had been.

BATTLING GRUDGES

Are your friends everyone's friends? Just because you get along well with a number of different faculty members does not mean that they get along with each other. When formulating your committee, it is important to try to ensure that the members will be compatible with one another. Keep in mind that your ability to befriend each member of your committee individually does not intrinsically mean that they are pals. Some educators find a dissertation defense to be the perfect opportunity to belittle the entire research field of the chair, raise old theoretical differences of opinion, or use it as an opportunity to seek revenge against the chair for some past conflict.

You may get along famously with each member individually. But, they may have longstanding arguments, conflicts, or outstanding debts that are bigger than your project and will likely last for many years in the future.

Beth discovered that her chair had taken a late sabbatical a few years earlier, which meant that other faculty had to teach classes that they had not intended to teach. Even though a few years had passed, one of those teachers still held a grudge. Beth knew that putting both faculty members on the same committee could be devastating for her, with each one revising and rejecting the work generated by the other person. She, therefore, decided to bypass the faculty member who carried the grudge. In the long run, it saved Beth a great deal of aggravation and possible delay in her dissertation project.

BATTLING BIAS

There is one other aspect of selecting committee members you know. And that is related to name recognition. If you plan to use your dissertation in the future in your job search, it helps to have a member who has a solid reputation in the area of your research. That kind of name recognition can perhaps open at least one more door to you in the future.

On the other hand, committee members may have their own political or academic agendas. For instance, Reid found that one member—Dr. Abbott—of his committee was also the chairperson of the department. The professor had a known reputation in the field. However, Dr. Abbott seemed to be trying to urge Reid to shift his research and the focus of his dissertation to coincide with her own current research interests.

"I felt like I was just doing her research," Reid said. "This didn't make me feel good, nor did I believe it was preparing me to be an independent researcher in the future."

Reid tried to enlist the support of his committee chairperson. But, because Dr. Abbot was also the chairperson of the department, Reid's dissertation chairperson did not wish to rock the boat with the woman who was also his own supervisor. The demands from Dr. Abbott persisted, creating ongoing tension between Reid and Dr. Abbott, as well as Reid and his dissertation chair.

Finally, although we would like to believe that people who have supported us thus far in education would continue to do so, that is not always the case. There are those individuals who see a dissertation as their last opportunity to "really teach you something" that you might not yet know.

For instance, Gerry was at the stage of preparing for his dissertation defense. He thought that he had good rapport among all of his committee members. Consistent with the standard in the field, he was asked to step out of the room prior to his formal lecture so the committee members could discuss privately if there were any issues that needed to be addressed as part of the defense.

In a comment that was intended as humorous, Gerry said, "That was a short lecture." After he excused himself from the room, one of the committee members was outraged by the comment, seeing it as disrespectful to the committee. He then took it upon himself to use the question and answer portion of the public lecture to place Gerry in the hot seat, asking grueling questions. Clearly the earlier affable atmosphere Gerry enjoyed were replaced by a very difficult defense because he failed to clearly read his committee members' attitudes.

WORK WITH YOUR CHAIRPERSON

The best advice we can give you is to work with your chair in selecting committee members. That will likely result in members who will work collaboratively with your chair and who will not use your dissertation as a forum for expressing their dissatisfaction with the chair.

It is important that your committee be composed of people who will work with each other (not against each other), return drafts of your documents in a reasonable period of time, and have an agreed-on goal as to the purpose of your project. Remember, if you have the wrong people on your committee, it can delay your progress and ultimately your graduation. Furthermore, it can make the process very painful.

Part V

Preparing to Begin

Chapter 19

Marriages Are for People, Not Work Products

Do not be committed to any part of a project that requires critical approval of a committee.

There is no doubt that in order to best perform a research project it is important to be invested in it. However, that does not mean you should be unbending in your adherence to the study. By this we mean that you are working with an adviser and a committee. These are all people who are bright, sharp-eyed, and have their own ideas about research, a dissertation, and how a research project ought to be conducted.

LEARN TO TOLERATE CRITICISM

One of the most difficult things to tolerate for any creative process is a critique. Whether it is your artwork, your home decorating style, your creative writing, or even a new outfit, it is extremely difficult to learn how to listen to the opinions of others. It is even more difficult to let their opinions change your personal actions. Be that as it may, part of being a professional is to endure the criticism of others, as well as to learn from such criticism.

There is no better opportunity than during the process of a thesis or dissertation to learn how to graciously accept the chewing up and spitting out of your professional writing. No matter how brilliant you are as a writer, you are still a student. While your adviser or your committee may recognize that you are a skilled writer, they are still likely to make suggestions for words or phrases. Therefore, our advice is to not be married to a specific phrase, comment, paragraph, idea, or draft.

Samuel was a relatively new and naïve writer. When writing a specific area in the background for his proposal, he was very pleased with his draft. He believed that the content seemed to flow just right. When the chair reviewed the document, he told Samuel that he didn't like the way it was written.

Samuel was hurt because he thought it was well written. He spoke to his classmate, Susan, bemoaning his frustrations that his chair told him to revise what Samuel believed was strong writing. Susan replied: "Isn't the goal to complete your degree while learning along the way? If your adviser thinks that the writing needs revision, wouldn't he know? Wouldn't it be easier to say, 'I didn't like it either; please teach me how to improve upon what I wrote?'"

Afterward, instead of arguing or defending his writing talent, Samuel agreed to rewrite the sections according to the recommendations of his adviser. That method smoothed the process and allowed for the project to move forward. It also taught Samuel what was working and what was not within his writing style. First, though, Samuel had to let go of his "love" for the words he had written.

IT'S ABOUT ACCOMMODATIONS

Working with a high-powered group of people inevitably means there will be critiques of your work and recommendations for changes. Josh wished to study differences in levels of self-confidence between children raised by one parent versus those raised by two parents. His primary measure of self-confidence was one he had developed as part of a prior study. As the study was coming together, one of his committee members, Dr. Harris, identified some mathematical problems with the questionnaire.

Dr. Harris noted that although the questionnaire might have been approved by a prior research team, the manner in which Josh was generating the summary scores violated measurement rules. Dr. Harris recommended using an already accepted measure rather than the new one created in the prior study. Josh was insistent that the questionnaire he had previously used be part of his dissertation. The committee member rightly pointed out that whatever results Josh might get for his dissertation will be tainted by using an invalid instrument.

Together they agreed that Josh would use a different measure as a primary one, but also include his own task so he could further study it once the statistical issues had been addressed. Of course it's easy to cry out, "It's my way or the highway." But, recognize that you will need to make accommodations along the way.

Jill ran into a snag in the dissertation process when she was rushing to meet a deadline. "One of my committee members was going to be out of town, so that resulted in a change of deadlines—moving it up," Jill recalled. "I sent a poorly organized draft of my proposal to the whole committee. However, the one member who was leaving town was the one who was personally offended by the proposal. She insisted that it be redone—and quickly."

Jill tried not to take this personally. "I humbly took the feedback and worked on repairing the relationship—and the proposal," She said. "I accepted it as my problem. If I had had the courage to ask for an extension of the deadline, I could have avoided this bump in the road."

Of course, it all goes back to who your adviser is and who is on your committee. Most of us accept criticism best when the positive aspects of our work are first acknowledged and then suggestions are given. If your adviser and committee members can avoid shaming you for any mistakes you make, it will ease your ability to listen to and accept their criticism. Furthermore, it is important to choose committee members who treat you already more or less as an equal. It is much easier to accept criticism when it is given in the context of a collaboration between two equals—rather than you being made to feel like you are an inferior being talked down to by a critical judge or an exacting teacher.

Chapter 20

The Runaround and Getting Your Ducks in a Row

> Get all your permissions and approvals from all persons and committees well
> in advance of when they will be needed.

The dominoes first need to be set up in the correct order before you can begin
watching them fall. Similarly, your research project will require you to get
appropriate approval from all necessary resources prior to beginning data
collection.

PERMISSIONS AND APPROVALS ARE NEEDED FROM VARIOUS PEOPLE AND COMMITTEES

There are the obvious individuals, including your committee chair and committee members, who will provide formal approval in the form of a proposal
defense. In addition, you will typically need to receive authorization from
your school or medical center's Human Investigation Committee (HIC) or
Institutional Review Board (IRB). Furthermore, the site where you will obtain the data will also need to provide some formalized agreement.

The difficulties that students encounter begin when approval is not lined
up in advance either by having the approval in writing or having obtained
approvals in the correct order.

For example, Antonio went to a juvenile court to obtain permission to
collect data from probation officers. The director of court services was enthusiastic about the project and readily gave him permission to discuss case files
with probation officers.

After the proposal was approved by Antonio's adviser and his committee, he went back to the director of court services to obtain written permission to collect his data. To his dismay, he found that the director had left the court to take a job in another state with another juvenile court. The new director was less than enthusiastic about the project and declined giving Antonio the permission he needed. Antonio was left with an approved project, but no place where the data could be collected.

Whitney asked a prison psychologist if she could interview sex offenders. The psychologist agreed, but the psychologist's supervisor was opposed to the project because of the perceived jeopardy to which Whitney might be exposed. The concern was understandable, and Whitney worked with her committee and the on-site psychologist to create a way to minimize her risk.

She returned to the supervisor at the prison with a revised project in which participants would be interviewed individually, in a secure area, and with the assistance of a second psychologist. The supervising psychologist was agreeable to the changes. Whitney was then able to move forward to seek formal approval from her school.

Dean had the written approval of the site where he planned to collect data. He was going to be having high school students first fill out a questionnaire. Then, Dean would go back and interview specific students who had answered specific questions in certain ways relevant to his study.

Dean had the approval of his adviser and his committee. All he had left was to get the approval of the Human Investigation Committee (HIC) at his college. But, the HIC rejected his proposal. When the HIC met with Dean, they had some very pointed questions about how the confidentiality of the participants might be compromised by the study. The HIC believed Dean could not guarantee confidentiality if he was going to identify some students for a follow-up interview. They requested changes that prevented Dean from carrying out the project he envisioned.

By first generating a project with your chair in conjunction with the supervisor of a clinical site—who might serve on the committee—such conflicts can be minimized. The HIC or IRB requirement of letters of support from the department and the data collection site prior to approval usually minimizes the runarounds that can occur.

Additionally, most IRBs or HICs provide templates of the various forms and the language researchers need to use. It is recommended that students always use those templates and follow them exactly. Furthermore, it is to your benefit to review your application to this committee with someone else who has been through the process successfully. That should help smooth the process and avoid any unnecessary surprises or delays.

Chapter 21

The Human Investigation Committee and the Institutional Review Board Hurdle

If you use human subjects in a research project, you will need the formal approval of the Institutional Review Board or Human Investigation Committee.

By federal Food and Drug Act regulations, an Institutional Review Board (IRB) or a university's or hospital's Human Investigation Committee (HIC) is designated to review and monitor all research involving human subjects. The purpose of an IRB or HIC review is to make sure that appropriate steps are taken to protect the rights and welfare of those who will be participating as subjects in the research. Depending on the rules of your institution as well as where your research is being completed, you may need approval from your local IRB, HIC, or even both.

An IRB or HIC has the authority to approve, disapprove, or require modifications in all research involving people, animals, or even microscopic cells stored from previously extracted tissue. Primarily focused on the protection of participant rights, oversight by these research committees also includes ensuring that protected information remains private, that data are stored in a secure manner, and that raw data as well as documentation of them are disposed of appropriately.

Some populations, such as children, cognitively impaired adults, and prisoners, are considered "protected populations." Special attention and scrutiny are made with research with these individuals to ensure that their rights are protected.

EVERY INSTITUTION HAS AN IRB OR HIC

Each university or hospital will have a formal group that meets regularly and reviews research project proposals. Thus, IRBs and HICs use a group process to review each proposal, ask questions of the researchers, and make suggestions for revisions before the group gives formal approval of the research project. As a researcher associated with a college or university, you will likely run into multiple review committees. One committee might be part of your school, while another committee might be associated with the facility where you will actually be collecting data. For researchers who may not be part of a formal institution, there are freestanding fee-based research review IRBs to ensure that studies protect the health and welfare of the research participants.

PARTICIPANTS MUST CLEARLY BE TOLD THE PURPOSE OF THE STUDY

One of the more important features of research with human participants is the need for people used as subjects to be informed about the purpose of the study, to be told what is required of them (time, effort, tasks, etc.), to be informed of the possible benefits, and to be told about any potential risks. This comprehensive document, the Informed Consent, must be approved by the IRB, as it is the document that will be given to each participant. They must be able to understand it and make an educated decision regarding their participation in the study.

Thomas proposed a research project involving giving personality tests to prison inmates. He had to present his proposal to his university's IRB. Thomas provided the committee with a rather long application form, also including a summary of the proposed study, the background for the study, and a detailed description of how information was to be obtained. Finally, copies of each of the questionnaires to be used in the study were submitted so the committee could make an informed decision regarding their use. As part of the application process, Thomas had to explain what benefits (if any) would come about through participation, and what tests would be filled out by the inmates.

The IRB asked Thomas questions about the Informed Consent. The prisoner representative (an IRB member who had special knowledge about prisoners and inmates) was concerned about the high level of reading skill required to understand the Informed Consent document. He was also concerned about other documents to be provided to prisoners and did not like one alternative, which was for Thomas to give a verbal explanation of the study. With the possibility of prisoners being placed in the position in which they might believe that they were required to participate, it was thought to be more appropriate to have a simplified Informed Consent at a fifth-grade reading level.

In addition, his school's IRB made several suggestions to Thomas, including that he clearly state the potential risks and benefits of participating in the study. They also asked that he make it clear that any inmate who opted not to participate would not be sanctioned in any way. Because they did not want Thomas's personal contact information provided in the consent form to allow participants to call with questions, the primary contact at the prison was to be used instead. Thomas made these recommended changes, submitted his materials the next month, and the IRB approved his final proposed research project.

Some studies do not require a formal written consent. Carol wished to evaluate the incidence of smoking on a college campus. To do so, she wanted to obtain access to the entire student body using an online survey instrument. A link to the survey was sent to all students in an e-mail. The first page of the survey provided a brief description of the questions to be asked, the purpose of the questions, and noted the student's ability to discontinue at any time. By clicking on "I read this and will proceed" at the bottom of the first page, the student gave consent.

THE PRIMARY PURPOSE OF AN IRB OR HIC

As can be seen in the examples above, the primary purpose of an IRB or HIC is to minimize the risk of legal, moral, and ethical violations that a research study might create. The thoroughness of the Informed Consent form in providing information regarding the time commitment, tasks required, challenges to confidentiality, and potential health or psychological risks is reviewed in this regard. Aspects of the risk of participation relative to the benefits of the study are weighed out.

The process involved in applying to an investigative review board (the FDA does not specify what name should be given to this board, although many go by IRB or HIC) is rather in-depth and thorough. Because the committee typically meets only once per month, if the HIC or IRB sees a need for you to adjust your project or the consent form, you will be held up for at least one month until their next meeting. Sometimes the changes will take longer, and sometimes, after modifications have been submitted, the board may ask for further revisions.

For instance, when Claudia submitted her revisions to the IRB, she had failed to specify how the students' responses in her study about suicidal thoughts among high school students would be kept confidential. In her proposal and in her Informed Consent she indicated that each student's responses to a survey would be anonymous and confidential. How would she assure this? Where would the response forms be stored? Would they be locked up, and who would have access to them? These were questions that the IRB needed answers to before finally approving her project.

IRB OR HIC APPROVAL MAY REQUIRE MULTIPLE FORMS OR MAY BE COMPLETED ONLINE

Applications to the investigation committee usually require completing a number of forms and providing a concise summary of the study to be generated. Although it is time-consuming to complete this information, the lack of this required approval could potentially delay commencement of data collection for many months.

Melissa, after earning her PhD, said she had a relatively easy time getting her university's IRB approval. "It was an online process at my college," Melissa said. "I didn't have any difficulty. However, I had the help of both my adviser and another student who went through the process successfully. I reviewed the application with my committee chair, and I used the templates the IRB provided on their website. By doing these things I had really smooth sailing."

Chapter 22

Managing Anxiety

> Look for support and strive to balance your life so that you are not overcome
> by anxiety and stress.

Some graduate students find solace, support, and motivation working in small groups that meet regularly. These meetings—which might be weekly or monthly—provide a set time to work, an opportunity to discuss any snags in the process, and a group of people from whom the student can seek advice for almost any aspect of the project—from data analysis to managing personality conflicts.

Although these groups can sometimes deteriorate into weekly socializing, a dedicated group can keep all members on track. You have a number of tasks required to complete even before you collect your first data point. Keeping to a weekly group meeting schedule allows you to set aside dedicated time, get support from your peers, and make use of the subtle pressure offered by your classmates in response to, "We are all going to work for four hours, how come you're not going to join us?"

Lydia worked in a small group in the early stages of writing her dissertation proposal. "It was helpful working with a group of bright students," Lydia said, "because in the beginning I was having trouble narrowing my topic. The wonderful thing about this group was they were able to take all the things I was interested in and everything I wanted to accomplish in my study, and help me form a researchable question."

Lydia, though, felt like once the group had helped her define the topic she wanted to research, that she was better off working on her own. She withdrew from the group and in retrospect believes that was the right decision for her.

A TRUSTED COLLEAGUE IS AN ALTERNATIVE TO A GROUP

An alternative to a support group is to find a trusted colleague who will provide "fresh eyes" for your project. As part of the writing process, you may wish to have a like-minded fellow student, a friend, or a colleague read your draft for content, copyediting, or both.

Brett decided to ask other students whom they would recommend as an editor. That led him to find an individual who had finished his PhD, but enjoyed helping graduate students with their dissertations. His adviser knew of this person and heartily recommended him as an editor for Brett.

"Hiring him was extremely helpful," Brett said after he had graduated. "It was helpful to me to have an unbiased set of eyes that could help me with the American Psychological Association style and required formatting."

Brett said that having an editor whom he was paying but who was familiar with the graduate program Brett was in was especially useful. "But, most of all," Brett said, "it was great to have an editor with professional knowledge who could let me know when things were not clear enough for a reader who did not understand the topic or when I needed to provide more information to better explain the model I was using in my research."

MAINTAIN YOUR MENTAL AND PHYSICAL HEALTH

While a study group or an editor can help manage your anxiety, there is also much you can do on a personal level that can help you maintain both mental and physical health while sustaining a high energy level. Most graduate students need to balance their life by establishing a routine of exercise, proper nutrition, and sufficient sleep. This will be particularly important if you are subject to high levels of anxiety, particularly when met with a large, drawn-out project.

Those readers who have been carefully paying attention will wonder why this recommendation seems so much in contrast to what we said back in Chapter 5. Yes, we said not to spend all of your time going to the mall or playing Xbox. But that was back when you had not started and you were using a cadre of techniques to procrastinate. Now that you are involved in a project that is up and running, it is alright to take a break in order to keep you fresh.

That being said, let's not get carried away! Going out for dinner and to a movie once a week is all part of the important socializing that should be your day-to-day life. Go out. Visit with friends. Watch television. Check in with your favorite social media websites. However, those activities should not take the place of sitting down and doing good work in order to complete what you need to complete—your daunting research project!

Fred said that managing his life while working on his dissertation was not particularly stressful. "I enjoyed the writing process," Fred reported, "and I actually liked the structure of having things to do at certain times."

The key, Fred said, was to stay organized. Fred exercised at the college's gym three times a week, practiced meditation, and tried to stay on a schedule to get plenty of sleep. "I ended up completing my dissertation well before most of my peers did," Fred said. "In addition to exercise and sleep, I set aside at least three specific blocks of time each week to work on the dissertation. I tried not to let anything interfere with those dedicated times."

"I'd go out with my classmates every Friday night," Fred said. "But, when they would get together on Saturday afternoons, I'd be reading and writing because that was one of my dissertation blocks. When I reached a stopping point, I would join them. By the end of one month, I had something to show for my four weeks of work while at the same time not feeling that I was removed from my friends."

Fred added one more thing that helped him manage anxiety. "Although I was immersed in my research topic, I tried not to worry or stress about what I needed to write next until it was one of those dedicated times each week that I gave over to working on the project."

Fred is a good example of a student who was able to balance his life during graduate school. Although he believed in regular exercise, he never let his need for physical activity become an excuse to avoid doing whatever he needed to do for his classes or his dissertation.

On the other hand, knowing when frustrations with school become too great to handle allows one to see the difference between "stress" and "crisis." Corinne felt anxious and under considerable stress throughout graduate school. "I was in graduate school nearly a thousand miles from my family," Corinne said, "and my mother was seriously ill during my second year of graduate work. I was really conflicted about staying in school versus going home to help care for her."

Her research project added to her anxiety. Often she was not getting enough sleep, continually worried about her mother, and she grew increasingly anxious about the amount of money she was accumulating in government loans. Her stressors clearly went beyond simply addressing her managing the tasks she had at school. Finding appropriate counseling, rather than simple friendships, helped Corinne work toward a balance of her academic life and that of her family's life so distant from her.

Part VI

The Project

Ins and Outs of the Process

Chapter 23

Managing Indifference

Find a balance between expecting others to regard your project as a priority with the indifference you may encounter.

Your research project and dissertation is likely going to be the most important thing in your life for several months or even several years. After all, it is necessary to complete your research project and the dissertation in order to reach your ultimate goal: Getting your degree.

HANDLING INDIFFERENCE

However, just because it is the most important thing in your life doesn't mean it will always be on the minds of your committee chair and the other members of the committee. At times, therefore, you may feel like the people who are supposed to be guiding you toward finishing your dissertation are apathetic or indifferent to your project.

Brittany felt at times that her committee lacked enthusiasm for her project. "I'd send a section of my dissertation to my committee and then wait sometimes for weeks before hearing from anyone," Brittany complained. "I'd be dying waiting to hear what they thought about what I had written and it would be like nothing. No response."

But remember, people who are serving on your committee are probably serving on other committees. They may also be teaching classes. Or, they may have their own research projects up and running. And, as you may hope for yourself, they could be busy writing professional journal articles, book chapters, or conference presentations.

And don't forget, even though graduate school has become the primary focus of *your* life, your committee members' professional positions are only part of their lives. Raising families, going on trips, and participating in local (nonuniversity) activities are all examples of how professionals spend their time outside of work. Just as you are encouraged to not work all day every day, do not expect your committee members to do so either.

When met with what might be seen as indifference and unresponsiveness, it may be because your project is only one aspect of your adviser's professional life. Because you chose competent and successful people to work with you, you have to expect they will be involved in continuing to be competent and successful. They could be working on their own research and writing, or they could be working closely with other students.

Furthermore, if you have been an absentee researcher for a period of time (e.g., you have spent one semester or longer away on an internship), do not expect your adviser to be more responsive to you than you had been active on your project.

After relocating to California from Illinois, David spent his internship year very methodically chipping away at the data analyses and writing his dissertation document. After eight months of slow and steady work, he e-mailed a draft of his final document to his dissertation committee chair. He gave out a deep sigh of relief, thrilled that his systematic approach to working a little bit every day finally paid off. His adviser responded the next day, thanking David for his work and telling him that he would be in touch soon. However, days turned into weeks and David became increasingly frustrated with his adviser's failure to respond.

"Why did I spend over one-half of my year working on this every day when he can't get back to me in a reasonable period of time?" David thought.

"Timely" feedback is subjective and the length of time for a response will vary based on the personality of your adviser or committee, the amount of material you sent out for them to review, the time of year, and even the interest of your committee in your project. Setting reasonable goals together with your adviser and committee will be a better tactic than sending a slew of documents or chapters followed closely by "friendly reminder" e-mail messages asking for feedback.

That's not to say that those friendly reminder messages aren't useful. Sometimes they are. Busy advisers and committee members may need nudging to call their attention to documents you previously sent that need their review. Simply make sure that the gentle reminders you are sending are being well received by those on the other end.

TAKE INTO CONSIDERATION THE SEASONAL PLANS OF YOUR COMMITTEE

Anna was surprised that she was unable to complete her dissertation while on internship. But, at the midpoint of the year, she decided that she would buckle down and get to work. She began taking weekends to run subjects and set up her database. Even over her spring break, she ran subjects and continued working on writing. As the internship year was ending, Anna began looking for a job. She was finally offered a position to begin on September 1, with the agreement that she would have completed her degree by that time. She pushed her dissertation into high gear. By June, she had completed her first draft and sent it to her committee.

But, Anna did not take into account the summer plans of her committee. So, although she was ready to complete her dissertation, the summer had begun and her priority was not the priority of her committee members. One member of her committee had even taken a summer teaching position out of the country. So what she saw as "indifference" might better be explained as Anna placing her needs above those of others—all without having taken others' lives into careful consideration.

Chapter 24

Managing Lunacy

Know when to work with a difficult or unreasonable committee member and when you need to cut your losses and take another tack.

Worse than an adviser or committee member who refuses to respond to your communications is one who continually responds in a manner that is negative, contradictory, or at odds with what was initially agreed on at the outset of the study.

Louis had an adviser who was absolutely wonderful. Louis described him as extremely supportive and helpful. He helped Louis pull together a challenging, but doable project. He also worked with him to get a strong group of faculty members to work on the research project. At his adviser's recommendation, Louis invited Dr. Willis to join his committee. An excellent researcher in her own right, Dr. Willis was well published in an area overlapping with the study Louis proposed. Unfortunately, that is where the difficulties began.

THE DIFFICULT COMMITTEE MEMBER

Dr. Willis initially provided mild critiques that were easily addressed in the proposal of the study. However, as the project moved from data collection, into the analysis and interpretation of the results, her involvement increased—and not in a positive way.

"She criticized everything I sent out," Louis later said. "She first complained that my results were wrong because they didn't agree with her published research. As a result, she tried to have me go back and collect another sample of subjects with more stringent criteria. Then, she insisted that numerous statistical analyses be performed as a way to generate findings that matched her publications."

As Louis become more frustrated, he went to his chair, who told him that he should grin and bear it, as Dr. Willis was a well-known researcher in the area. However, when Louis tried to write up his formal dissertation, Dr. Willis complained that the writing was not clear. She kept returning drafts of the document. Sometimes, she offered editorial corrections; other times, she would put an X through an entire page and write "rewrite!"

Louis was particularly astounded when comparing drafts and seeing that a paragraph she absolutely hated was one that she had insisted Louis add after she had read an earlier draft.

"I tried to defend myself against Dr. Willis," Louis remarked. "But even after she approved each section, she would later change her mind and say it wasn't finished. On a few occasions she stated that I should start over from scratch."

What seemed obvious to Louis was that Dr. Willis did not like the findings from his study and was taking out her frustration on all aspects of the project. Unfortunately, this situation from a committee is not that uncommon. Frustrations and conflicts of committee members' experience are sometimes inappropriately taken out on the graduate student.

COMMUNICATION AS AN INTERVENTION

The first line of defense against unreasonable requests, confusing feedback, contradictory suggestions, and other difficulties is communication. Louis met with his committee member several times to try to bring about a better understanding between them. He wanted to get clarity from early on as to what Dr. Willis really wanted from him—and how he could best achieve that.

He attempted to bring about a clear structure of responsibilities with Dr. Willis in which she had a specific role to play in giving him feedback. Louis also agreed to provide her with outlines of the activities he accomplished, his goals, and even drafts of his work. But none of these efforts were successful. As time went on, the demands became greater. His attempts to provide clarification seemed more like an opportunity to be berated than supported.

The first line of protection against unreasonable requests and revisions is communication with the concerned committee member. Attempt to arrange a clear structure of responsibilities with the individual, seeking appropriate guidance from your chair. Provide outlines of activities accomplished, goals, and drafts of prior work.

If speaking with a frustrated member of your committee fails, then speak frankly with your chair or some other faculty member to seek guidance as to how to deal with unreasonable requests from that particular individual. When no other option seems to provide satisfaction, then it is time to cut your losses early and *run*. If you get a lot of push-back when in the writing stages of a proposal, don't think that passing the written document will be any easier.

Finally, Louis met with the chair of his committee. He spoke candidly about his inability to create a positive working relationship with Dr. Willis. He sought guidance from his chair as to how he was to deal with Dr. Willis's unreasonable demands. Considering how much difficulty she was causing just in the writing of his dissertation, things were not likely to get better when he had to go through a defense with her in attendance.

Given that Louis tried various reasonable strategies to work with Dr. Willis, his committee chair—quoting the song by Kenny Rogers—said that often in life it was important to know "when to hold 'em and when to fold 'em." This was a time to fold 'em, his chair advised. He could not continue to work with her and expect to finish his dissertation without considerable anxiety and stress.

In the end, the committee chair gave Louis his support. He had reviewed the early discussions and realized that no good outcomes resulted. He now agreed that Louis should cut his losses with Dr. Willis and find a suitable replacement. Louis was concerned that cutting Dr. Willis out of the committee might have a negative consequence when he would later look for jobs in the field. Understanding his concern, Louis was assured by his adviser that it would be unlikely that Dr. Willis would be in a position to influence his future. He nonetheless offered to speak with Dr. Willis on behalf of Louis.

Louis replaced Dr. Willis with another committee member. The remainder of the committee approved the change and allowed the new member to proceed even though that individual had not been at the proposal meeting. Louis was then able to complete his dissertation along with his dissertation defense in a timely manner, with suggestions and advice that were productive.

Part VII

Approaching the Defense

Chapter 25

No Surprises—Certainly Not During the Proposal or Defense Meetings

Doing your work on the front end will make your proposal presentation and research defense much easier to handle.

You have already effectively incorporated the information we have provided thus far, so this chapter may be irrelevant for you. However, there will be some graduate students who enjoy suspense and believe that their committee will as well. Take it from us, they don't.

THE PUBLIC DEFENSE

Perhaps at this point we should explain what a thesis or dissertation defense is and what it normally entails. The research defense aims to accomplish two main goals. First, it provides an opportunity for you to present your dissertation as a final step in recognition of your completed doctoral work. Second, it provides an opportunity for your adviser and your committee to evaluate and formally discuss your dissertation.

The dissertation defense is a very important moment in a graduate student's career. The defense is when you deliver an oral presentation of your dissertation to your adviser, your committee members, and any guests you choose to invite. Some schools encourage all members of a research team to attend while others encourage all students and faculty to attend. This way the presenter has some support and those on the team get a sense as to what is required before they are standing in the same place.

GIVE YOUR COMMITTEE ADEQUATE OPPORTUNITY TO READ YOUR DRAFT

If you have failed to keep your committee apprised along the way, then you must at least give your committee members sufficient time to read your draft. As discussed before, just because you are ready does not mean that your committee members are suddenly ready to drop everything to read your paper. So make certain that you are not dumping a draft of your dissertation on them only a few days before your actual defense.

Typically, you will have had a plan of what you were intending to do. But, once the numbers arrive, there may be a different way of looking at the same information that could better address what you wished to study. A request to have you perform additional work is not a punishment, but should be seen as collegial support.

A DRAFT IS A DRAFT

Your draft of the document has been sent to committee members. Notice that the word "draft" is used. Don't think that it is completed simply because you have finished it. A review of a scientific research project is not simply reading a paper. Faculty members who are invested in your study will do more than that. Of course, there will be the copyediting and grammar changes which can be quickly addressed.

However, the larger issues relate to the evaluation of the data and the interpretation of the analyses. A good committee member will take the time to make sure that the design of your study was performed as planned and that the way in which the results were analyzed was done so in the most informative manner.

David was very excited about getting to the end of his project. His data had been collected, and he carefully did all of the required analyses. After meeting with his adviser on a number of occasions, he obtained guidance and returned to the data to conduct additional analyses. He excitedly completed that work, soon engaged in writing his final document.

As is the case in most schools, in order to participate in graduation David needed his accepted paper to be submitted two months before graduation. The deadline for submitting the final document rapidly approached. David and his adviser were quite confident that the document would be completed one week before the deadline, about two weeks after their last meeting. So, David scheduled his defense for that week.

Unfortunately, although David diligently worked on his project and got guidance from his counselor, neither one considered the time commitment or investment to be made by the other reviewers. So, when one of his readers noticed that a different statistical technique was needed than the one used, David's excitement about being done with his project changed to nervousness about what else he might need to do.

Furthermore, another reader took issue with the conclusions. She recommended that a revision offer additional references to articles supporting an alternative interpretation of the data. That was when David's nervousness turned to panic, aggravation, and frustration.

Was the timing anyone's fault? Not really. The only issue was David's assumption that he could finish quickly as the deadline approached. The first lesson David learned was to make sure that there is plenty of time to address concerns prior to a defense date.

LEAVE TIME FOR FEEDBACK FROM THE COMMITTEE PRIOR TO YOUR DEFENSE

As noted above, it is important to have a conversation with your committee members. Although preferably in person, some advisers are happy to provide feedback by e-mail or phone. Regardless, these interactions are important to address any suggestions made before you are walking into your public lecture. These meetings will at worst require revisions to your work and at best give you insight into questions to be asked in the defense.

MAKE SURE THERE WILL BE NO SURPRISES AT YOUR ORAL DEFENSE

More important, though, is the potential risk at which you place yourself by not speaking with members prior to the defense meeting. You do not want to have any big surprises at this oral defense. One reason is that you are nearing the end of your graduate work and you probably (we could even say you most definitely) do not want any snags in completing your graduate degree.

But if you invited your family (say, your mother and father) and friends, you certainly don't want to be embarrassed. This is why we strongly recommend that you send copies of your dissertation out ahead of time to your committee and that you meet with each of them to find out their concerns. At the end of your presentation, you should be able to anticipate what each committee member will say or what each is likely to recommend.

Candace, for instance, did not meet with each member of her committee. As a result, when it came to defend her dissertation, she was extremely anxious. "I felt confident that I had conducted a rigorous clinical trial and at that point in my education I realized how unusual that was for students in my graduate program," she said. "But I had no idea what my committee thought and what kind of questions they would ask me during the defense."

Unfortunately, the document that she presented had not been approved formally by the committee members. Her tables were not in standard form and the faculty had difficulty understanding the results. Each committee member thought that the other had approved the style. Candace was excused from the room after her presentation and a long discussion ensued regarding the sloppiness of her work.

The committee chair apologized and took responsibility for not having kept a closer eye. But, that did not change the fact that the style was unacceptable. She needed to make significant revisions to the document.

Candace said that since she hadn't talked to her committee members before the oral defense, she was not sure what questions they would ask or how—or if—she would be able to respond. The greater issue turned out to be something even more essential to her research than the presentation.

Meeting informally with your committee chair and each of your committee members will prepare you in completing your final document and also for your public presentation of your work. Most students, like Candace, may spend weeks or even months thinking about and preparing for their defense. It is a relatively simple matter to meet with each committee member to find out what they think about your dissertation. That interaction allows you to be prepared and there should be no spontaneous questions or criticisms you won't be able to handle in stride.

JUST ASK FOR FEEDBACK AHEAD OF TIME

If you want to feel less anxious and more confident, then eliminate any potential surprises by asking for feedback ahead of time. Do this at least a couple of weeks before the date of the defense so there is ample time to make any recommended revisions. Once you've sent it out to your committee, follow up with e-mails asking for appointment times to sit down and discuss their reactions to your dissertation. Scheduling an appointment time will ensure they actually read it. And, of course, they will be able to voice any concerns or reservations they have. That will also allow you to address during your defense any part of your dissertation that may be troublesome to a particular committee member.

Chapter 26

Preparing for the Defense

> Coordinate with your committee members and work with your adviser to get
> the project and oral presentation in final form.

As you begin seeing the finish line approaching, you must remember that you
will not make it to the end if you slow down. There are more practical issues
that need to be addressed in order to get you to the defense (public lecture) of
your research project.

SCHEDULING THE DEFENSE

As obvious as is similar information discussed elsewhere in this book, you
need to make sure that there is a date and time for your defense. When it
comes to scheduling a time for a proposal meeting or a final defense, you will
be met with the challenges of trying to satisfy the demands of multiple
calendars. Your committee chair and your committee members are busy
people with many demands on their time.

Therefore, you should start planning well in advance so that you can find
a suitable time that is convenient for everyone. That won't be easy, so make
sure you allow enough time for this. And as mentioned before, just because
this is crunch time for you and you want to be completed, that doesn't mean
the committee will be jumping up and down as much as you. They have their
own scheduled priorities to manage that will get in the way of your own
interests.

For example, Brent was beginning to work on the final draft of his dissertation for his social work PhD At that time, he met with his adviser to select a time frame for the defense. "I sent an e-mail to all of my committee members," Brent said, "asking them for their availability during a three-week window."

After Brent received replies from his committee, he sent a new e-mail, which proposed several times that might work for everyone on his committee. "The defense date was really selected by a democratic process," Brent said. "The most popular date was selected and there was enough time for everyone to do any adjustments of their schedule so they could attend."

After that hurdle was past, Brent met again with his adviser to reserve the room and the equipment he wanted to use. The adviser and the School of Social Work took care of announcing the defense date and posting flyers in the department.

Because of the difficulty in managing schedules, there are some online schedulers that are being used. Particularly when individuals on a committee are not in the same location, having access to a communal calendar can be very helpful. With this calendar, the "owner" of the schedule posts all possible times for a meeting. Then, they send a link to the schedule by e-mail to all of the other individuals on the committee.

Each member goes to the website and indicates all of the times that are acceptable. Once all members have put in available times, the owner of the schedule can see what times are best for everyone. Consideration should be given to using such a system particularly as individuals are more likely to be available online than in person.

PREPARING YOUR PRESENTATION

Once your dissertation is written and the defense date scheduled, you will then need to prepare for your defense. Find out what others at your school have done in the past with regard to handouts, slides, and presentation style. But most important is to seek guidance from your adviser as to the length, content, and style of your presentation.

Some schools want you to present the entire study in a public setting as if it were a "job talk." This model requires you to stand in the front of the room and provide a 45- to 60-minute presentation in which the background of the study, method used, results obtained, and interpretation of the findings are provided.

The "job talk" style also comes with the expectation that you will have appropriate audiovisual aids to accompany your presentation. The question and answer session following a job talk will generally be open to the public. In such a setting, committee members wait to ask questions until the public has completed their inquiries.

Other schools select different models of presentation, including having a meeting with mostly your committee only in which you present the methods and statistics only. In those cases you are to avoid any interpretation of your findings, so that information can be used in response to questions posed by the committee (e.g., what do these data mean? What are the implications? What suggestions do you have regarding further areas of study? What could you do differently if you had this same question to answer?).

Kristina said that her adviser was very helpful in providing guidance in her preparation for her defense presentation. "He provided me with an outline of what to include in my oral presentation, the suggested length, and examples of what other graduate students had done in their presentations," Kristina said. "He let me make decisions about the actual style, and, of course, I was responsible for putting it all together. He reviewed my outline of the presentation and he suggested a dry run with other graduate students," she said.

In fact, her adviser pulled together the research laboratory team and had Kristina present her dissertation as if it was her actual defense. She discovered areas in her talk, such as when providing background, when she went on too long. And she discovered which prepared slides were too busy or too repetitive to be useful.

"Doing a sample run-through was very helpful because having done it once, I was much more comfortable with the presentation," Kristina said.

But don't stop there. If you did it once, fine. But, maybe you will need to do it again. Even if it is by yourself at home, do your full presentation aloud as if you are in front of an audience. Such a practice presentation will allow you to make sure that your visual presentation is accurate and that you have the slides in a format that works.

Chapter 27

You Know More Than You Believe You Know

Whether you really feel this or not, you are the expert on your dissertation. Nobody knows the material better than you.

No matter where one is in their professional career, they may be hit with the imposter syndrome. The imposter syndrome is when individuals who are learned, experienced, informed, and knowledgeable fail to see those attributes in themselves. They will minimize what they know, assuming that others know more than they. Experience that they do have will be sloughed off as not entirely relevant. Or they will view their knowledge as not being sufficient to really understand their particular area of study.

While you are reading this text, you will still assume that others know more than you. Even more so than a professional who is already working in the discipline, you are probably a bit afraid that others know more than you do. After all, you are a graduate student—and not yet a professional.

Yes, it is true that you have been led to believe you do not know enough to perform some activity. That's the nature of being a graduate student—indeed, it's the nature of being a student. There are professors and other experts whose books and work you read who know things. You are just a student. And by definition, a student is someone who studies. The definition says nothing about a student being someone who has knowledge or is capable of imparting knowledge to others.

LOOKING AT REALITIES

Put away that negative thinking! Even your adviser likely suffers from the imposter syndrome from time to time. So, it is time for you to take control of what you know and what you believe. As you prepare to make your public presentation, deep-six your own "nay-saying" and take control of that which you know.

Go into your presentation and dissertation defense with self-confidence and a "can do" attitude. The reality is that you have gotten this far. You have completed (or nearly completed) your course work. You have researched and written your dissertation. You may have conducted an original research project. Through your own doing, you convinced your adviser and your committee to accept your plan for your dissertation. Now you are approaching the final step: Defending the work you have done. And that's all this is—the final step in a process. And you can do this just as you've done all the rest of the steps in this journey toward a doctoral degree.

Who wrote the background for the study? You did. Who compiled and analyzed the data? You did. Who wrote the first draft of the document (and the second draft)? You did.

At this stage of the process, you will realize that no one has read your work product as closely as you have. Even your adviser, who is likely quite familiar with your project or your research, will not be as intimate with the subject information, data collection, and analyses as you are. It is you, the neophyte researcher and dissertation writer, the person who has slaved over each data point, statistical analysis, and written word, the person who read every book and journal article in your subject area, who has morphed into who you are today: the expert on your area of study and your dissertation.

YOU WILL BE ANXIOUS GOING INTO YOUR DEFENSE

Of course you will be nervous preparing for and anticipating standing before your adviser, your committee chair, and assorted family, friends, and colleagues. There would be something wrong if you weren't anxious. But that shouldn't immobilize you. Instead, it should motivate you, just as it helped Shannon to prepare harder.

"Due to my level of anxiety," Shannon said a few months later, "I took time off from work to make sure that I was as prepared as possible. I knew that the defense had to go well, so it was necessary to put aside work responsibilities and concentrate on my presentation. That helped my confidence, because I knew I was doing everything possible to be successful."

By going over her dissertation many times, preparing a PowerPoint presentation, and practicing that presentation in front of friends and classmates,
Shannon was ready when the day arrived for her defense.

LEARNING FROM THE EXPERIENCE

Like Shannon, you will learn from the experience of having to defend your
dissertation.

"I learned that I could withstand extremely high levels of anxiety with
poise," Shannon said. "The feedback I got from my mother, who knows me
better than anybody, as well as from other people, was that I didn't look
nervous. Of course, nothing could be farther from the truth."

But, Shannon felt like the graduated (not "graduate") professional she
would soon be. "I felt validated following my defense," Shannon remarked.
"There were so many times during graduate school that I doubted myself or
had questions about whether this was the right field for me. Surviving the
defense and having it go as well as it did helped me see that everything I
worked so hard to achieve was the right course. I had what it takes to be
successful in my chosen career."

WHAT HAPPENS IMMEDIATELY AFTER THE PUBLIC
PRESENTATION?

The process at many universities is that after the formal presentation and a
question and answer session, the student leaves the room and the committee
discusses the defense and identifies any concerns they have. With the right
amount of preparation ahead of time, you will feel confident leaving the
room, having mastered not only the entire project but also the public presentation. You should be walking out with confidence!

While the committee is meeting to discuss the presentation after the fact,
the student along with family and friends will wait patiently for the results.
Family, friends, and other invited guests will offer hugs, huge compliments,
and effusive congratulations. The student will be justifiably relieved that this
part of the process has ended.

What goes on behind the closed door? In most cases, the faculty will be
discussing the progress of the student and completion of their degree requirements. Other times, they will be so wrapped up in the discussion of the
project, and other potential spinoff projects, that the issue of the defense

becomes secondary. We have sat on committees in which the members are so excited about the topic area that after 15 minutes someone sheepishly asks, "Do you think that we should have the candidate come back?"

On rare occasions, and only for those who didn't do their preparation ahead of time, the committee will discuss the weaknesses of the project, what the student will need to address, and by when the student will complete the required tasks.

After a few minutes—sometimes it is as few as five minutes, though at times it can be somewhat longer—the student is asked to come back to meet with the adviser and committee. If things have truly gone well, then the committee will simply offer their congratulations. Be aware that quite frequently there will be editing changes that need to be made prior to full acceptance. That should not come as a surprise. What is really exhilarating, though, is that when you return to the room to face your adviser and committee, they will address you as "Doctor."

Chapter 28

The Ruler Lady

You need to learn as much as you can about the technical requirements for the final preparation of your dissertation. If you don't adhere to the strict guidelines your university probably has for dissertation formats, your work will be returned for revision until it is right.

WHO IS THE RULER LADY?

The Ruler Lady (although to be fair, it could be a Ruler Guy) is the person in your graduate department who knows every rule when it comes to submitting your final documents. And that person is the one who will literally take out a ruler to ensure that your margins are acceptable according to the university requirements. Don't underestimate the power of the Ruler Lady. She can send your dissertation back to you until it is completed in exactly the way she—and the university—requires.

Despite your adherence to the publication styles through the American Psychological Association or the University of Chicago, everything is off the books when it comes to your school. Every university has its own unique rules and regulations that guide the presentation of the final product. Even if APA style says to double space your reference list with tabs indented, your school might require spacing of 1.5 lines and a hanging tab. Learn the local rules!

There is often one individual with rubber finger guards who will examine every page to ensure that you have adhered to the requirements relating to the measurement of the margins, font size, font selection, paper weight, line spacing, order of sections, reference style, and so on. As irritating as this process might be, the frustration can be avoided—or at least minimized to some degree.

Clearly the last 20 years have eliminated many of the hassles previously experienced when manuscripts were generated by typewriter. But the issues of the size of the margins, acceptable fonts, and the weight of the paper have not reduced any of the scrutiny devoted to the placement of tables, the spacing of text in the appendix (which might be single spaced although the rest of the document is double spaced), and the location of the page number.

ONE FORMATTING PROBLEM CAN DELAY COMPLETION

Caitlin was a wiz with her word processing program. She had no difficulty with the basics of creating and formatting a document. She also was one of those few people who integrated the references feature of the program, so she could have a reference list at the end of the document and simply indicate where in the document each reference would appear. Happily preparing to submit her final document prior to the dissertation defense, she became increasingly more frustrated with a single annoyance.

Her school wanted running heads on the upper right corner for most pages. But, at the beginning of each chapter, the university required the page number to appear centered at the bottom of the page. Try as she could, Caitlin could not get the References in the end of the document to allow a different footer than the rest of that section. In the end, she simply typed a single page document, emulating the text from the References but forcing the page number to go where it was mandated.

Annoying? Of course. But, not as problematic as it might have been had Caitlin submitted the document and it were rejected for the formatting issue.

HOW TO DEFEAT THE RULER LADY

As boring and as mundane as this may sound, it is important. How important is it? Well, it may be the absolute final hurdle you have to negotiate before completing your PhD And failure to learn the minutiae can prevent you from completing your dissertation or getting your PhD—at least for a period of time. Compare this to a high school student who arrives on a Saturday to sit for the ACT or SAT. Known around the school as being the top in his class, he failed to bring a pencil to complete the test. Forgetting to bring the appropriate #2 pencil makes him as "knowledgeable" as the student who did not show up at all. In other words, if you don't follow the rules, no one will ever know the outcome.

Know the rules. They are public domain and easily available from your school. The earlier in the process you do this, the better. After all, some dissertations can run to several hundred pages. Save yourself enormous headaches at the end and do this early on.

Along the same lines, there are dates and deadlines that the university adheres to. Don't rely on your committee or any friends or faculty members to know all these deadlines. Find out on your own and then mark them boldly on your calendar.

THE FINAL REVISIONS

Manny was given a few minor corrections by his committee following his defense. "I made those by the next day and submitted it to my adviser," Manny said. "The committee didn't even need to see the final draft as they left it up to the adviser. It was after that that I went through the arduous process of submitting the final, approved dissertation to the graduate school. I remember thinking more than once, as it got returned to me three times: Just when you think it's over, there's always just one more thing."

But when Manny got an e-mail that the final draft had been accepted and the degree was posted to his transcript, he felt it was a good day. "There was this surreal feeling," Manny recalled, "that I had just completed my PhD after three rugged years of working on that project. It was a good day—no, it was a great day!"

Like Manny, once you've learned the rules, there should be few revisions needed after your defense.

Part VIII

Publishing

Chapter 29

Authorship

Inclusion and order of authorship can become a sticky issue, despite professional organizations and universities that have clearly stated guidelines.

If you are reading this book prior to completing your dissertation, then you will probably blanch at the idea of ever finishing your project. Even more remote is the possibility that you will spend time trying to get the paper in shape for publication. Be that as it may, you will likely have conversations with your adviser about the possibilities of submitting your dissertation (or portions of it) for publication or as a paper or presentation at national conferences. Further, faculty members often have an area of research that you have jumped onto with your study. So, with almost all projects, you should consider that it will be publishable in some form.

Just when you thought that difficulties with publishing were related to the complexity of your study, other difficulties can rise up and can, therefore, be addressed with a bit of foresight. Possible areas of conflict should not be avoided until after the defense. They should be addressed early in the process—perhaps even months before a final draft of your dissertation proposal is started.

WHO GETS A BYLINE?

One of the first potential areas of conflict is authorship. Who will be the main author of any papers or articles that come about as a result of your work or your research? Who will be other authors listed at the top of articles, poster sessions, or presentations?

After reading this chapter, you should be more aware of possible authorship problems. Therefore, you need to begin a conversation with your adviser very early in the process. Be aware that ethical principles promulgated by the various professional organizations clearly state the criteria required for authorship on a publication—especially when the project is related to a thesis or dissertation. In addition, universities similarly have rules and regulations regarding the order of authorship between adviser and graduate student.

While not every graduate student will be familiar with the ethical standards of the major organization in their field, those standards and guidelines are frequently referred to by professional authors because of their broad and extensive application. The reasons why professional organizations and universities address authorship are quite apparent. Not only do many professionals, especially academics and scholars, build their reputation among their peers on the basis of their publications, but also publications often play a significant part in employment, promotion, and tenure.

GUIDELINES ON AUTHORSHIP

In many disciplines and fields collaboration is the norm, and authorship can be controversial. That's why guidelines have been established, not only by the American Psychological Association (which has a model set of ethical standards), but such groups as the American Chemical Society, the U.S. National Academies, the American Mathematical Society, and even journals themselves. For example, there are authorship guidelines required for manuscripts submitted to journals.

In the social science field, authorship is defined very narrowly. And the uniform requirement for manuscripts submitted to biomedical journals is that in order to be considered an author one must have satisfied all three of the following conditions:

- Contributed substantially to the conception and design of the study, the acquisition of the data, or the analysis and interpretation;
- Drafted the article or provided critical editing in the revision of the article;
- Provided final approval of the version to be published.

The medical community is a bit more "liberal" in their inclusion of coauthors in the byline of a paper. Perusal of medical journals will easily demonstrate how those journals offer authorship to all professionals included, even tangentially, with a project.

In general, authorship entails a public acknowledgment of scientific or professional contributions to a publication, and the contribution includes involvement in various tasks associated with the project. Different professions may have varying standards of what is required, but going to your discipline and your school is paramount in finding the correct level.

GRADUATE STUDENTS AS AUTHORS

As a graduate student, conducting research and publishing your work is often essential. It is likely critical to your professional development and the advancement of your career. Therefore, many students decide to try to publish their dissertation or the results of any research that contributed to their dissertation. It is generally accepted that a student is listed as principal author on any multiple-authorship articles that are based on the student's dissertation.

On the other hand, there are times when a graduate student will work closely with an adviser as a research assistant on a funded grant project. The adviser provided the idea, the data pool, and even the know-how to analyze the obtained information. Should that make the student the first author? Probably not. In fact, that situation would make it less likely to have the student in the coveted first author position. But, the only way the issue can be discussed is if it is discussed freely and honestly.

Theresa was a master's student who created a project with the assistance of her adviser to interview grade school children. She then developed the project, obtained permission from school districts, and submitted materials for IRB evaluation. Once approved, Theresa gathered the data, analyzed the numbers, and wrote her thesis. Her adviser was helpful in aiding interpretation of the findings and in editing the manuscript. After successfully defending her master's thesis, Theresa's adviser recommended that it be submitted for publication. He said, "Let's put my name first on the paper, as I have published already and that will help us get this new paper accepted." What that adviser did violates almost all professional organizations' rules. When graduate students know what is and isn't acceptable can help avoid conflicts before they occur.

OTHER AUTHORS

Additional authors may have their names attached to the article that results from a student's dissertation. However, the contributions and ideas of other authors ought to be discussed and agreed on very early in the process. But in order for any individual to be listed as an author, they must have made substantial contributions to the research or the article.

Some journals now request and publish information about the contributions of each listed author. In addition, some journals list the role of other individuals in an acknowledgment section if their contribution does not rise to the level of that of an author.

Jack was an undergraduate student, new to the idea of research. He happily took on the role of research assistant in a lab, under the direction of an upper level graduate student. The graduate student was doing a project under the direction of a faculty member. Jack dutifully performed all tasks he was supposed to do as a research assistant. He collected data, scored them, and entered the findings into a computer database. The graduate student showed Jack his proposal to be submitted to a professional meeting.

Jack couldn't help but notice that his name was not included as a coauthor. But rather than shy away from the conflict, he explicitly asked the graduate student in charge if Jack could be added as a coauthor. It was explained to Jack that performing grunt work, although very important for any project, is not the same as making a professional contribution. While not happy with the answer, without asking the question he may have resented the student without having appropriate information. He was appropriately included in the acknowledgments when a full version of the paper was published.

RESOLVING CONFLICTS ABOUT AUTHORSHIP

A quick Internet search about authorship issues will guide you to some of the worst examples of problems in this area. For instance, there have been legal cases in which graduate students have successfully filed suit for plagiarism against their former advisers. There have been other cases in which faculty have lost their jobs for publishing material collected in their laboratory as part of a student's project. At the other end of the spectrum, there have been schools who have reprimanded students for not appropriately including their own adviser on the research generated from that adviser's laboratory as part of the graduate student's dissertation.

Just like a good marriage, success is best accomplished though communication. When writing an article with one or more people, talk about authorship in the beginning, just as you discuss other aspects of the project. If authorship is discussed and agreed on right at the start of the project, problems and conflicts are likely to be resolved.

These conversations should include not only order of authorship. But they should also lead to decisions regarding the contributions to the overall project of everyone on the research team.

IF ISSUES ARE NOT RESOLVED EARLY IN THE PROJECT

However, if issues of authorship aren't resolved early on they can become much more significant issues later on when it is time to submit the article to a journal. In the event that you and your colleagues cannot resolve the issues that have arisen over authorship, it may be helpful to consult your adviser as well as your university's guidelines for authorship.

Finally, not only do some colleges require the chair of the dissertation committee to be a coauthor, but some also insist that all committee members be included in the byline. Students might even use the promise of coauthorship as an incentive for an individual to become involved as a committee member. Whenever there is a conflict over authorship, consider a compromise. For instance, a compromise could result in inclusion of an individual as author for a conference presentation, although not for a published article.

Chapter 30

Finding a Journal

Choosing the right journal for the submission of your first article can be daunting, but there are suggestions that can help you be successful.

Appropriate placement of an article based on your dissertation can be as daunting as trying to determine the correct statistical analysis of a complicated research project. And typically graduate students have critical questions when they begin the process of publication: Which journal will accept my article for publication? What would be the best journal for my article? How do I go about finding the right journal? Should I publish in the best journal or in the journal that will give the easiest acceptance?

CHOOSING A JOURNAL

Journals are generally ranked within a field in terms of the difficulty of getting published and in terms of the breadth of readership. Experienced authors may aim for a specific journal for various reasons.

For instance, one particular journal may add to the author's prestige within the field. There are some professionals who may have only a handful of articles. However, if such papers are all published in journals with broad readership, that raises the significance of those publications. The journals *Nature* or *Science* would fit in this category.

On the other hand, a different journal may be more specific to one field. So, the readership may be smaller, but it is more focused on an "inner circle" of individuals.

In addition to considering the best home for an article, one also has to take a look at the relative benefit of some journals over others. It is clear that some journals are more stringent in their acceptances, while others have a lower bar set at what is thought to be acceptable. Further, some journals may be appropriate simply because other papers in a specific area of study have all been published in the same journal.

As a graduate student submitting your first journal article, you may have your heart set on a specific journal because it seems that the best articles appear in that journal. You may believe that having an article in this journal will get your career off to a rousing start. However, there are certain considerations that need to influence your selection of the first journal to approach.

Experienced authors may submit first to the best journal in their field knowing that although acceptance would be a long shot, still they are willing to risk rejection. They may believe that taking the chance with the best journal is worth any delay rejection will entail.

PRACTICAL SUGGESTIONS

Here are three questions followed by practical suggestions to use as guidelines in deciding on which journals to approach:

1. Which journal has published articles similar to the one you've written? Find those journals and carefully review their submission guidelines. Once you are familiar with submissions guidelines, follow those guidelines in submitting your manuscript to the one journal that has published the most articles similar to your article.
2. Which journals have theme issues each year (or on a regular basis) in which your article would possibly fit? Some journals have special themes and will be looking for articles that meet the criteria for these special theme issues. If your article relates closely to a theme, then by all means submit it as soon as possible before the issue is filled up.
3. Which journal appears most frequently in the reference section of your research, dissertation, or article? If your article cites other articles which have been published in a particular journal, then it could mean that your article may be especially relevant to the journal and the editor of this journal tends to accept articles similar to your article.

DON'T BE AFRAID TO SUBMIT YOUR ARTICLE

It doesn't matter that the editor of the journal to which you'd like to submit your work has never heard of you. Journal editors are less interested in your name and more interested in the quality of your manuscript and your writing. In fact, many journals have blind reviews in which the individuals evaluating the articles do not know who wrote the papers. If you have a valuable contribution to your field, the editor will give your work fair consideration.

If you are not sure about the appropriateness of your paper for a particular journal, don't be too afraid to e-mail the editor-in-chief or the managing editor to ask. A simple abstract, or even just the title, might be sufficient to allow the editor enough information to see if the manuscript is appropriate for the journal.

A PROFESSIONAL-LOOKING ARTICLE

Although submissions are mostly performed electronically these days, most editors can immediately spot the novice submission versus the professional submission.

Be sure to follow the submission guidelines exactly. Many editors won't review articles that have not been submitted properly. For instance, if the guidelines call for using APA (American Psychological Association) style, then make sure you familiarize yourself with APA style and follow it rigidly. If the guidelines call for sending eight copies, send exactly eight copies.

In general, you are more likely to be treated like an experienced author if you submit material that looks professional. A professional-looking manuscript will have these qualities:

- The manuscript has a clean and neat appearance.
- There are no obvious typographical errors and this includes an absence of spelling errors.
- The article is printed in a standard font (such as Times New Roman), it is in 12-point font size, and it is double-spaced.
- It includes a cover letter addressed to the editor.

If your manuscript includes everything just discussed, it will be treated with greater respect and is likely to be given fair consideration.

Chapter 31

The Reviewers Said *What*?

When you send your article out to a journal, expect criticism. Use this feedback to make your article more effective and more likely to be published.

When you submit an article to a journal and the editor believes it may have some value to the journal's readership, it will be assigned to reviewers. Often it will be sent to two or more reviewers for impartial reviews.

The reviewers will read your article critically. Their primary task is to make sure it is a scholarly article that has been appropriately evaluated, and that it will provide a significant contribution to the field. They will evaluate the background of the study, making sure that you provide a reasonable rationale for why the study needed to be done in the first place. The actual work you did will also be assessed, including the subjects used, measures included, and procedures employed. Did you sufficiently describe the analyses? Are the results presented in a usable format? Are the figures and tables appropriate? Are they excessive? Are they absent?

Once the careful evaluation of your paper has been done, as it was with your public defense at a time of greater anxiety, the reviewer will make recommendations about whether that particular journal should publish it. Reviewers might accept a paper outright. On the other hand, they may reject the manuscript altogether because they believe that the paper is not appropriate for the journal, does not provide sufficient background, has faulty analyses, or does not have a large enough sample size. A fortunate researcher will have reviewers respond to the editor with suggestions for improvement, offering a recommendation to *revise and resubmit* the paper, or to *accept pending revisions.*

When these reviews are completed, they are returned to the editor, and the editor, in turn, will send them to you. Usually, those reviews are accompanied by a cover letter from the editor who will either indicate acceptance, rejection, or the need for revisions of your article.

The responsibility falls to the editor of the journal to evaluate the reviews and reach a decision. If the reviewers reach different conclusions from each other, editors might make a decision based on their own analysis. Alternatively, they may seek another reviewer to assist in better understanding the strengths and weaknesses of a submission.

FIRST, THE BAD NEWS

It is the rare manuscript that is accepted "as is" for publication. In fact, to add to the bad news, the average rejection rate for journal submissions hovers at about 70 percent. Therefore, you are more than twice as likely to receive a rejection letter than you are to receive an acceptance letter. So, expect that you will be rejected when that notification comes back from the journal where you sent your manuscript.

NOW FOR THE GOOD NEWS

Even if you get a rather terse rejection letter, you will probably get copies of the reviewer's comments. These comments will provide you with specific details about why your article was rejected. It may be painful to read the cold and maybe even (at least it might seem so to you) heartless destruction of your article.

However, the reviewers are often right. That is, they will have pointed out specific reasons as to why your manuscript was just not right for this particular journal. Or why the paper in its current form is not ready for publication at all. The reviewer's comments will let you know what parts of your article did not meet their standards. But having the benefit of these critical reviews gives you some options. You can use the criticisms to revise the article so that it can be resubmitted to the same journal. Or, you could opt to send it off to another journal—either with or without substantial revisions. But be warned, if your area of study is small enough, your paper may be sent to the same person reviewing for another journal.

Usually the reviewers make valuable suggestions for how the article could be revised. Their recommendations might require extensive reworking of the article (or even the original research). While no author looks forward to being told their article needs a great deal of work in order to get published, this feedback does provide a better idea as to what you have to do to get it accepted at some journal.

WHAT IF YOU RECEIVED A CONDITIONAL ACCEPTANCE?

If the editor says they would consider your article with some revisions, you know exactly what you have to do. Revisions requested by a journal can range from minor grammatical changes to the inclusion of an additional sample of participants. Simply put, your choices fall into three categories:

- Revise and resubmit to the same journal
- Send it to another journal
- Throw in the towel on getting the paper published at all

When you choose to revise and resubmit, you will need to explain how you handled each comment made by the editor. Although a reviewer might request an additional analysis to be performed or theme to be discussed, the editor will highlight those aspects of the article that *really* need to be changed. There are also times when the recommendations made by the reviewers are not feasible (such as adding a different measure) or affordable (such as getting a new sample from another country). In response to the editor, you can explain why a recommendation might not be changed in the revision. Just because the editor or the reviews say to do something, doesn't mean you should accept their judgment without offering a counterpoint.

If you choose to revise and resubmit, you should carefully consider every point made by the editors and reviewers, and make sure you address each of these concerns in revising your article. Make your corrections and revisions in a timely manner and send it back. Include in your cover letter how you have handled the recommended revisions and how your manuscript is improved.

If you decide to try another journal, such as the next journal you consider to be a backup journal, you cannot ignore the reviews already received. There is almost certainly some gold in the comments by the reviewers, and that journal's rejection of your paper does not invalidate the concerns raised by the reviewers.

You may not be willing to do the kinds of revision that the editor requires. If you are not willing, then you can submit your article to another journal or you could throw in the towel and perhaps accept that your article may never get published.

IF YOU DECIDE TO DEEP SIX IT

You may decide that for various reasons you cannot make the revisions required and that you would rather forget about a revision and give up on this particular article.

Still, you cannot ignore either the editor's or the reviewer's comments about your manuscript. What they said may be especially useful for the next article you write and submit to a journal.

You may give up on an article—there's no shame in doing this. Every serious writer or researcher has had to deep-six an article or even a book.

But if you give up on an article do so with the acceptance that the editor and reviewers were correct. And don't let the criticism and rejection beat down your determination or desire to get an article in print. It is, of course, humbling to have an article rejected, but it's not the end of the world. You can do other research projects and write other articles.

But if you truly believe the editor and reviewers were incorrect in the assessment of your manuscript, then step back, review it for ways you can fine-tune the article, and send it out to another journal.

Chapter 32

Editors and Reviewers Are People, Too

Editors and reviewers may not recognize the significance of your contribution to the field. That may mean you need to try another editor and another set of reviewers at another journal.

Lots of things can happen when you submit your article to a professional journal:

- You may not hear anything for two years,
- The reviewer's comments may seem way off base,
- Reviewers may say opposite things and may even contradict each other,
- The editor or reviewers simply didn't get what you were trying to do or say.

LOOKING BEHIND THE CURTAIN

Just as in *The Wizard of Oz*, there is just another human making decisions about manuscripts that are being submitted. The editor (a human) is reading the reviews that have been written (by humans) to identify strengths and weaknesses of your paper. Even good quality, well-meaning editors make mistakes.

One of the authors of this book (BNA) found a significant statistical error in a published paper. After writing a brief article explaining the error and providing the corrected tables, he submitted it to the journal. Within days, the editor of the journal sent a rejection letter stating that the article was "not appropriate for the journal." Not appropriate? Incredulous, outraged, and appalled, the author let a few days pass.

A colleague suggested that the author call the editor to ask, "How could a corrected document for a paper published in your journal not be appropriate?" The call was made. The question was asked, but without as much sarcasm as would have been used on the first day. "Oops," said the editor. "Wow. We really messed that one up. Don't worry. The paper will be accepted once the figures are double checked. If you are correct then we won't even send it out for a formal review."

WHY HAVEN'T I HEARD ANYTHING?

Articles can get lost or misplaced. That can—and does—happen. If you haven't heard from the journal in a reasonable amount of time, e-mail, call, or write to ask if your manuscript was received or if the reviews are still pending. You can ask when you might expect to get an answer about acceptance. Most journals usually give you some idea in the submission policies and guidelines as to about how long it takes to get a reply. If they do provide this kind of information, and that amount of time has come and gone, then contact the editor.

The other author of this book (JW) sent an article to an editor. After not hearing anything for four months, he got enough courage to call the editor. A secretary took the call and assured him that the editor would read the article "this weekend." More time went by and again he called, and, again, talked to the secretary. This time the secretary admitted it hadn't been read—and in fact they couldn't find it. She asked that another copy be sent and they would give it priority. It was sent; they did give it priority; and it was subsequently published.

THE REVIEWERS WERE SUPPOSED TO BE EXPERTS, BUT THEY FAILED TO GRASP THE SIGNIFICANCE OF MY ARTICLE

That can happen, too. Reviewers are typically experts—but not necessarily in every facet of your field. Since they are human, they can make mistakes or simply miss the importance of your article. If you think that happened, send it off to another journal and hope that the editor and reviewers at the next journal are somewhat more savvy about the area you've written about.

If a journal rejects a good paper, does that make them wrong? Not necessarily. You might have a great idea and excellent data, but you have not presented it in the best way to get your idea across. If their comments indicate that you failed to address an issue that you believed you actually addressed, then the issue might not be the reviewers. It might still fall to you to better highlight that particular issue.

THE REVIEWERS' COMMENTS WERE POLAR OPPOSITES, BUT THE EDITOR WANTED ME TO REVISE THE ARTICLE FOLLOWING WHAT THE REVIEWERS SUGGESTED

Do you need clarification? Get in touch with the editor and ask for clarification and help. Editors are often very approachable, particularly if your article interests them and they would like to see it resubmitted. Maybe you're missing something in what the reviewers said. Or, maybe the editor didn't quite understand that the reviewers had contradicted each other. Or, maybe the editor agreed with the first reviewer and disagreed with the second reviewer; he really only wanted you to make changes based on the first reviewer. Most editors will try to clarify what they would like you to do next.

WHY AM I MISUNDERSTOOD?

Editors and reviewers are so human that sometimes they miss the mark completely. You may have written an article that is ground-breaking and is a significant contribution to the field.

Arguing your case with the editors may be helpful, but there are plenty of other journals, too, that might see your article for its true significance. Send it off and hope you strike gold with the next journal. But, as noted above, the issue might be that your writing has not sufficiently argued your case for the importance of your paper.

Part IX

Collaborating

Chapter 33

Making a Team

Collaboration and teamwork is very valuable in any discipline.

You may enjoy working alone. You may also believe your best work comes about in some solitary pursuit. But, step back and see if there are other ways for you to excel in your profession. Research and making contributions to your field of study is not necessarily about showing yourself to be the best, the brightest, and the most important innovator in your field.

Of course, if you really feel that researching, writing, and publishing is a competitive sport, then go for it. And go it alone if you must—in the process demonstrating to everyone how brilliant and talented you are.

But the fact is that research, writing, and making significant contributions to your field can be enjoyable—and it can be collaborative. The faculty in most universities is already aware of this. That is why professors work with a team that includes a number of students, both junior and senior graduate students. Others are brought into the research team gradually, learning from those already there, while at the same time moving forward the professor's overall area of study.

When Richard was a graduate student, he worked in a research team with other graduate students. They all reported to the same faculty member, who was really the head of the research program. Richard began his first year of graduate study, listening to the work generated by those ahead of him in the program. By his fourth year, he completed his master's thesis, had an idea of his dissertation project, and had taken the lead in many aspects of the daily functions of the lab. Once he completed his dissertation over the next year, he was thrilled about the possibilities of not having to be responsible to others. He no longer needed to teach people new to the field, double check the work of others, or otherwise tend to the research lab.

However, within the next few months, Richard began to recognize that despite the extra work placed on him to be part of a group, he also received knowledge, manpower, and even motivation to do more from a group. His research contributions had certainly been unique and innovative. But, they were also generated because he had been part of a larger group.

Collaborations with others can take many forms. Some people work well sitting side by side at a computer screen, analyzing the data, writing the document, and revising it together. They use the time together generating ideas, keeping each other on task, and creating enthusiasm for their project. Other people like to work alone, sending a complete version to their colleague or coworker for evaluation, revision, and a return back to them. The style of how you work with others will depend on who you are—and with whom you are working. What works for you? We can't answer that. But, we can encourage you to try various forms of collaboration so you can find that out for yourself.

INNOVATIONS OFTEN COME FROM COLLABORATIONS

Not to belabor the obvious, but some of the most innovative discoveries, theories, and inventions came about through collaborations. For example, Charles Darwin worked with his mentor Charles Lyell, Marie Curie and Pierre Curie worked side by side, and Picasso and Braque collaborated to develop cubism. And the famous quote from Isaac Newton reflects how he felt about collaboration: "If I have seen further than others, it is by standing on the shoulders of giants."

Collaborations thrive on diversity of perspective and constructive dialogue that occurs between individuals. Just look at journal articles these days—and we don't care what field of study you are in or which journals you choose—and you'll see that a majority—an overwhelming majority—of articles in leading journals are the result of collaborative efforts among several people.

TEAMWORK LEADS TO NEW IDEAS

The lone innovator. The eccentric inventor. The solitary genius. These are pretty much anachronisms these days. Today, it's all about working with other professionals and collaborating by bringing together different ideas and a shared knowledge base. It is intense interaction and the merging together of diverse perspectives that leads to new ideas. In other words, it's all about teamwork.

If you can work with your colleagues; if you can share ideas; if you can bring together your respective strengths; if you can collaborate as a team; then you are an invaluable professional who will make any team with which you work stronger and possibly more innovative.

While working on a specific project, each member of the team will have some responsibility. By simply having a "homework assignment" you will be sure to keep more active in the study. The likelihood of taking some time off to work on another project will diminish once you have committed yourself to perform a task for your cowriters. The tasks may not be large, but any work on a project will keep the project active in your mind—and keep the momentum going.

As a graduate student, you are already well on your way to being an effective collaborator. You've been meeting with your adviser as well as working with your dissertation committee. And very likely any articles that come about because of your dissertation will include a collaborative relationship.

Enjoy this first collaboration and look for further opportunities to share your ideas and talents with others.

Chapter 34

Who Is Doing What on the Project?

Reach an agreement on these issues at the start and the project will proceed much more smoothly.

Like most students, when you started on this journey called "getting your PhD" your most pressing goal was to successfully complete the dissertation process so you could get your PhD and begin your career. In order to reach the goal of obtaining a PhD, you had to work with an adviser, a dissertation committee, several professors, fellow classmates, and, if you had to complete an internship along the way, a supervisor and temporary colleagues.

And what did you learn from working with all of these people?

Perhaps the most important skills you picked up from all of these working relationships were learning to manage conflict and get along with diverse people with different perspectives and unique goals. But you did it. And, as it turns out, these newly acquired skills will serve you well in the future, particularly with any ongoing research projects.

The difference once you have graduated with your doctoral degree is that when you get involved in research and writing projects you will have greater control in deciding with whom you wish to work. Although there is certainly more freedom in selecting your research partners, a clear understanding needs to be at the top of your agenda when you set out on a new project with collaborators.

With the idea of considering collaboration firmly in place (see Chapter 33), you will need to work with others to formulate the right kind of plan. One of the benefits of the process you endured for months—and very likely years—is that you acquired a set of skills you never expected to acquire. You need to take that knowledge of how to get through a big project, and apply it as a "team leader" in your next project.

As you learned in a previous chapter, it is important to decide authorship before anyone does any work. In this chapter, we are bringing to your attention the equally important aspect of clarifying the specific tasks that are to be performed by each member of the team. In most writing or research projects, there will be various tasks that have to be assigned to various team members. These tasks may include writing a proposal or a grant, planning the research, obtaining Institutional Review Board approval for the project, deciding on the statistical program to be used, interpretation of the research results prior to writing, and journals that should be targeted for the study. And, very important, the tasks will include deciding who will be designated as the overall project director.

An additional concern that needs to be discussed early in the project is the manner in which the writing will be done. Both authors of this book have worked with numerous coauthors, and each project is different in terms of how the writing is shared and coordinated. Is one person going to be responsible for the first draft? Will different authors write different sections? Will one person write the final draft? Will there be regular writing meetings when all authors work together on each section?

If all of these concerns are addressed right in the beginning, then the project can proceed much more smoothly.

Part X

Wrapping It Up

Chapter 35

Congratulations! You Did It! Now, Where Do You Go from Here?

The knowledge acquired in managing your research project can be applied in other areas.

You survived your dissertation! That's terrific! You are part of a select minority who start—and finish—their dissertation. There are many students who do not complete their PhD program. That is, they give up before completing their dissertation and, thus, they never receive their PhD But you are different. You demonstrated hard work, perseverance, tenacity, and courage. But where do you go from here?

COMPLETING YOUR DEGREE IS NOT THE END

You accomplished something that is significant, but it is not the end. It is the beginning. With a doctoral degree in hand, there may be many opportunities in your field for you to get the position you want at a salary that will allow you to start paying off your student loans. But there may not be all those opportunities that you envisioned. However, there will be opportunities for fellowships, postdoctoral internships, and other chances to continue to enhance your education and keep learning.

Many people, at all levels of academic achievement, view the earning of an advanced degree as the final destination. We believe it is simply the beginning of a lifelong pursuit of education and new knowledge. You are a specialist, but there is plenty more to learn.

RESEARCHING AND WRITING

We happen to think that researching, writing, and publishing is a wonderful way of continuing to learn and continuing to demonstrate your professional competence. Many people, having achieved their PhD, are eager to be hands-on professionals, working with the problems and the thorny issues in their field. From our point of view, though, no matter what you choose to do as a professional, you should never stop learning.

Remaining active in professional literature is a unique way of continuing to push yourself toward new knowledge and understanding in your field.

And you will be able to apply the knowledge you have acquired as a researcher to other areas. When reading professional journals or listening to a lecture, you will be able to bring with you the critical eye required to evaluate all research. Did the authors collect the right type of data? Are the measures they used valid? Is the presentation an accurate discussion of their findings? How easy would it be to apply their results to your own day-to-day work?

WHAT IS YOUR GOAL?

No matter what your goal in your field, be aware of your goal and strive to reach it. You already demonstrated that you can set a very lofty goal and reach that goal. Now you can set new goals to accomplish in your area of expertise. Always set new goals and always strive to reach those goals. They may be more far-reaching goals—to be an outstanding leader in your field, to research an important area, or to write a book—but have goals and dreams and always pursue them.

You have not simply completed a huge requirement for a degree. By this time, the skills you learned have become incorporated into your professional "soul." You can access these skills in the future, whether or not research becomes your passion. You haven't simply jumped over all of those hurdles, you have indeed become a member of the profession. Welcome.

FINALLY

Finally, you have reason to celebrate your most recent accomplishment. But once you have celebrated and received congratulations from family, friends, and colleagues, set your sights on ventures and new dreams. Take pride in what you did, but continue to reach for the stars with the confidence that having survived your dissertation gives you.

References

American Psychological Association. (2010). *Publication Manual of the American Psychological Association* (6th ed.). Washington, DC: Author.

Davis, G., & Parker, C. (1997). *Writing the Doctoral Dissertation: A Systematic Approach.* Hauppauge, NY: Barron's Educational Services.

Recommended Resources

1. *The Dissertation Desk Reference: The Doctoral Student's Manual to Writing the Dissertation* by R. L. Calabrese (2009).
2. *The Elements of an Effective Dissertation and Thesis: A Step-by-Step Guide to Getting It Right the First Time* by R. L. Calabrese (2006).
3. *Writing the Doctoral Dissertation: A Systematic Approach* by G. Davis and C. Parker (1997).
4. *Finish Your Dissertation Once and for All! How to Overcome Psychological Barriers, Get Results, and Move on With Your Life* by A. Miller (2008).
5. *Surviving Your Dissertation: A Comprehensive Guide to Content and Process* by K. E. Rudestam and R. Newton (2007).
6. *Dissertations and Theses from Start to Finish: Psychology and Related Fields* by J. D. Cone (2006).
7. *The Dissertation Journey: A Practical and Comprehensive Guide to Planning, Writing, and Defending Your Dissertation* by C. Roberts (2010).
8. *Completing Your Qualitative Dissertation: A Roadmap from Beginning to End* by L. Bloomberg and M. Volpe (2008).
9. *Completing Your Doctoral Dissertation or Master's Thesis in Two Semesters or Less* by E. H. Ogden (1997).
10. *Writing Your Dissertation in Fifteen Minutes a Day: A Guide to Starting, Revising, and Finishing Your Doctoral Thesis* by J. Bolker (1998).
11. *Writing the Successful Thesis and Dissertation: Entering the Conversation* by I. Clark (2006).
12. *Writing the Winning Thesis or Dissertation: A Step-by-Step Guide* by A. Glatthorn (2005).

13. *Demystifying Dissertation Writing: A Streamlined Process from Choice of Topic to Final Text* by P. B. Single and R. Reis (2009).

About the Authors

Bradley N. Axelrod, PhD, is director of neuropsychological and psychological assessment services at the John D. Dingell Department of Veterans Affairs Medical Center, where he has been since 1990. Dr. Axelrod has published extensively in the area of psychometric analysis of neuropsychological and psychological test measures. He provides clinical training to psychology interns and medical residents. In addition, he has provided research support to graduate students, serving on numerous master's thesis and doctoral dissertation committees. He is an adjunct associate professor in the Department of Neurology at the Wayne State University School of Medicine and in the Department of Psychology at Wayne State University. He has served on the Department of Veterans Affairs Clinical Investigation Committee since 1993 and the Wayne State University behavioral review board for six years. He authored over 120 professional articles and 13 book chapters, and made over 180 presentations at scientific meetings for psychology and neuropsychology. Dr. Axelrod has served as a reviewer for over 20 research journals within the behavioral sciences. He is a fellow in the Neuropsychology Division of the American Psychological Association, a fellow of the National Academy of Neuropsychology, and a fellow of the American Board of Professional Neuropsychology.

James Windell, MA, has been court psychologist in the Oakland County Circuit Court's Family Division, in Oakland County, Michigan, doing group therapy with delinquents and divorced coparents with high conflicts. He is also an adjunct instructor in the Criminal Justice Department at Wayne State University. He has authored or coauthored 15 books in the areas of parenting, medicine, high-conflict divorce, and various other areas. He has had a weekly newspaper column for more than 25 years. He is the editor of *The Michigan Psychologist*, the quarterly newsletter for the Michigan Psychological

Association. Mr. Windell has appeared on more than 175 radio and television shows, including both local and national talk shows, and as a parenting expert he has been frequently quoted by literally every parenting and women's magazine. He has served on the Institutional Review Board at the University of Detroit–Mercy for several years. He has worked closely with PhD graduate students and has assisted several in conducting their research and completing their dissertations and publishing their results in professional journals. He has been a member of the American Psychological Association's media panel for 20 years.

Other Titles of Interest

OTHER TITLES OF INTEREST BY
ROWMAN & LITTLEFIELD EDUCATION

*From Student to Professor: Translating a Graduate Degree into a
Career in Academia*
By Carol A. Mullen

*Passing the Leadership Test: Strategies for Success on the Leadership
Licensure Exam*, 2nd Edition
By Leslie Jones and Eugene Kennedy

Advancing Your Career: Getting and Making the Most of Your Doctorate
By Michael Brubaker and Dale Brubaker

Total Leaders 2.0: Leading in the Age of Empowerment
By Charles J. Schwahn and William G. Spady

Getting It Right: The Essential Elements of a Dissertation
By Raymond L. Calabrese

Creating Positive Images for Professional Success, 2nd Edition
By Patsy Johnson Hallman

Edwards Brothers Malloy
Thorofare, NJ USA
December 14, 2012